Tudor
Dolls'
Houses

Geoffrey West

The Crowood Press

First published in 1999 by
The Crowood Press Ltd
Ramsbury, Marlborough
Wiltshire SN8 2HR

British Library Cataloguing-in-Publication Data
A catalogue record for this book is available from the British Library.

ISBN 1 86126 130 6

Acknowledgments
With thanks to Clive and Georgie de la Nougeréde of Dolls' House Junction,
West Wickham, Kent (0181 776 0248), and to Kristin Baybar of Kristin Baybar,
Gospel Oak Village, London (0171 267 0934), for their help and support.
These specialist dolls' house shops stock a very wide range of accessories.

Typeset by The Florence Group, Stoodleigh, Devon
Printed and bound by Leo Paper Products, China

Contents

1

Types of Building

When Henry VII won the Battle of Bosworth Field, he ended the dangerous and politically turbulent period of English history known as the Wars of the Roses. He was also able to exert some control over his powerful subjects, who, in turn, were better able to maintain order throughout their own principalities. In medieval times, the era preceding the Tudor dynasty, larger towns were walled against attack, castles proliferated, and there were violent disputes between adjacent magnates, not to mention aggressive incursions into the English border towns by the Scots. Architecture for the rich and influential had to be defensive, and this philosophy filtered downwards, so that even more humble dwellings had an element of defence, exemplified by the crenellated tower houses.

Henry Tudor, the first of the successful Tudor monarchs, created a stable govern-

Fig. 1   Box frame construction – vertical studs full height of each storey wall.

ment and kept England aloof from foreign wars, making the Tudor period (1485–1603) a time of steadily growing prosperity and relative peace. The architecture reflected this: affluence and stability meant that yeomen farmers could build larger homes, secure in the knowledge that these properties would be inherited by their children, and would be safe from the ravages of civil war. There was a wave of new architectural ideas, some of which still hold good today. A newly-built house which was recently featured in a magazine was designed and built with a Tudor exterior, using reclaimed material from demolished buildings of the period. The result was both authentic and pleasing: it was designed with modern living in mind.

There are a number of practical drawbacks to living in a genuine Tudor or medieval building today. People were shorter in stature in past eras, so anyone above average height has to duck under ancient ceiling beams. Insulation is virtually non-existent and difficult to introduce, and modern necessities such as electric wiring and pipe-work are hard to hide. Walls were originally designed to dry naturally from the inside as well as outside, at complete variance with modern heating technology. The timber frame can settle in alarming ways, causing internal plasterwork to crack without warning, and the many nooks and crannies can be impossible to light successfully and are even harder to keep clean. Staircases can be cramped and dangerous, making the

Fig. 2   Side view of timber-framed house showing jetty and oriel window.

Fig. 3   (below) Frontage showing large jetty overhang.

movement of large items of furniture difficult.

Fortunately, none of the above problems apply to dolls' houses. In fact the very facets that make these buildings attractive yet impractical, are ideal for re-creation on a small scale, and the quaint and original features can be a source of endless individual invention. Georgian dolls' houses look best if they are expertly constructed with much attention to detail, whereas the Tudor style requires a fondness for eccentricity rather than a high standard of precision. Ideas can spring to mind in the middle of a project and can be incorporated without major upheavals; similarly, something which looked good on paper might not be a success and can be scrapped with only minor difficulties. The period encompasses a range of styles that should appeal to anyone who is drawn to the romance of old buildings, and wants to make something truly individual.

For most people, the Tudor period of building is synonymous with timber-framed houses, but there are many other

Fig. 4   Corner view showing timber beams.

styles, from stone-built country cottages with thatched roofs, to grandly imposing buildings for the gentry, referred to in those days as 'halls'. The bare bones of a timber-framed house and a Tudor galleon look similar, and this is no coincidence: shipwrights were also house-builders.

MEDIEVAL AND TUDOR WOODWORK

A great deal of medieval England was covered by forests, and at the start of the fifteenth century there were four million acres of woodland. So unlike today, when building timber should ideally come from a sustainable source, the material was plentiful and cheap, and its use was encouraged, so as to liberate tracts of land for cultivation. In fact, up until the seventeenth century, most English towns were comprised of timber-framed buildings. For strength and durability, oak couldn't be beaten, and was used mainly for richer homes in the first part of the period, but was gradually introduced to smaller dwellings during the second half of the sixteenth century. The unseasoned timber was allowed to season whilst in position, which accounts for the familiar sagging, warping and twisting effects that occurred, and are considered as part of the charm of some of the still-surviving examples.

Mathematical principles, developed by Euclid and Pythagoras, allowed carpenters to mark and carve accurate joints, promoting their craft to a highly developed science. The carpenters' workshop and yard were known as a 'framynplace'. The timber-framed structure was constructed on the ground, the joints and components being identified with special numerals and marked up accordingly before the frame was dismantled, to be reassembled on site. A scribe and a scribing compass were used for the marking process.

FROM TREE TO TIMBER FRAME

Trees were felled with a narrow axe, but sometimes a broad axe was used first if the tree was large. The trunk was then split

Fig. 5   Gable wall showing timbering.

7

with an axe and iron wedges into baulks, which were cut to length with a twart – a cross-cut (across grain) saw with a handle at each end to be used by two men. Pit saws were also two-handled two-man saws, and were used for cutting large logs, with one man working from underneath in a pit, the other from above. The great pit saw was similar to the twart but longer and with larger teeth and cut *with* the grain – a rip saw. The framed pit saw had a narrow blade fixed in the centre of a large rectangular frame to keep the blade taut and was mainly used for cutting boards.

For structurally important house timbers, for example corner posts and huge transverse beams, the trunk was shaped by the broad axe and finally trimmed with an adze, a kind of axe with the blade set at right angles. Smaller timbers, known as scantlings, such as were used for studs (vertical wall posts) and floorboards, were produced by cutting the baulks across their length, using a pit saw.

JOINTS

Most joints were mortice-and-tenon, meaning that a slot (mortice) was cut from one piece of timber to exactly the same dimensions as the tenon (tongue of wood) shape at the end of the other piece, and the two were slotted together. Tenons were cut using a one-handled, curved-blade handsaw, whilst mortices were formed using a mallet and chisel, or by making a series of holes with an auger (wood-cutting drill), the remaining bits being chipped away. The assembled joints were secured with heart-of-oak pegs called trashnails that were inserted through previously-bored holes. Iron bolts, screws and nails were too expensive to be used, which was fortuitous as the acid within unseasoned oak would have quickly corroded them. The trash-

nails were not used on first assembly, since it was necessary to make allowance for final adjustments when the entire structure was complete. Instead, hook pins – long tapering wooden pins like tent pegs – were used and not driven in too far, so that they could be withdrawn for adjustment before the final assembly with trashnails. These pegged joints were, and still are, extraordinarily strong.

CONSTRUCTIONAL DETAILS OF EARLY TYPES OF BUILDING

THE CRUCK

The original cruck construction was one in which two adjacent trees were bent so that their tops could be lashed together. The same thing was done to another two adjacent trees a few yards away, and the top unions of the pairs of trees were joined by a horizontal trunk laid across, to form the roof line. There was no distinction between roof and walls, whereas more sophisticated buildings had a roof as a separate structural unit. Unfortunately, only those crucks that were built for the rich now survive, as these were made of superior timber.

Since trees were rarely so conveniently positioned, the early crucks were comprised of pairs of inclined poles (blades), with one end set into the ground, the top ends lashed together either at the apex, or just below, so that they crossed. With a pair of blades at each end, and maybe one or more in the middle, these apex joints were connected by means of a lighter pole, called the ridge beam, along the complete length. Pairs of blades had to have a match-

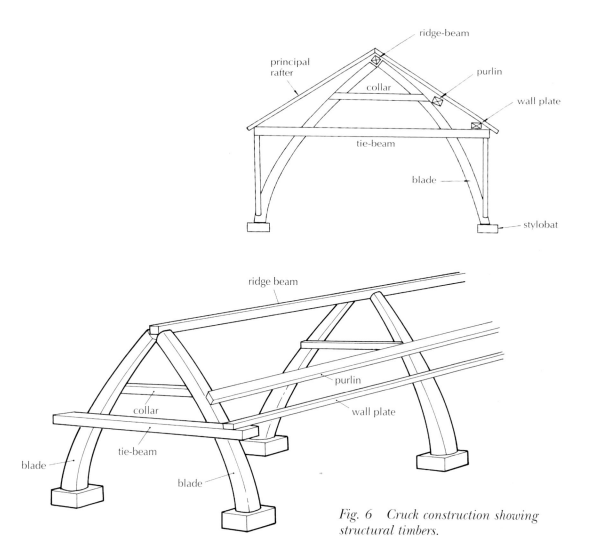

Fig. 6   Cruck construction showing structural timbers.

ing curve and were often cut from the same tree to ensure this. A simple cottage might have just two cruck frames.

Originally the blades were burnt at their ends (presumably to create a protective charred layer) and set into the ground, but later they were set on stone foundations, called stylobats. The apex juncture formed a cleft for the ridge beam. The distance between pairs of blades was referred to as a bay, normally, but not necessarily, sixteen feet long. Fixed from cruck frame to cruck frame were horizontal timbers called purlins, on which the roof rested. To prevent the feet of each pair of blades splaying outwards, a tie-beam was attached between them, approximately six feet from the ground, and was fixed to the blades

9

Fig. 7   Brick infilling between beams.

with oak pegs. Entry to the building was through one of the triangular ends, the surrounding gaps closed with a timber framework filled with a blend of twigs, wood and cow dung, known as wattle and daub.

Two-Storey Crucks

From being one-storey, crucks were later divided horizontally to create an upper floor. At first there was little headroom in the upper storey, but longer tie-beams were then introduced, the ends joined vertically to the foot of the blades by posts, thus forming a more stable structure. To support the upper storey, horizontal wall plates were laid on top of the triangulated tie-beams, and these wall supports ran from bay to bay. The ends of timbers were fixed to the wall plates, and studding (lines of vertical timbers used to create a wall) attached to these; the upper storey was thus independent of the roof structure.

   A horizontal collar gave additional structural stability to the blades, and was fixed close to the apex. Sometimes another collar was fixed lower down, to give greater support to the purlins on which the roof rested. The roof of a two-storey building had a shallower pitch, requiring a duplicate blade or cantilevered bearer to support the lower purlins. Dispensing with the tie-beam, to allow for more headroom, meant that bearers called cruck spurs were needed for wall-plate support.

Other Types of Cruck

There were two kinds of genuine cruck: the full cruck, with blades starting at ground level and meeting at the apex, and the raised cruck, where the blades still met at the apex but began part-way up a wall. In addition there was the jointed or scarfed cruck, where one blade was vertical and the other bent, plus the raised base or truncated raised cruck, where only the centre (curved area) was used. An upper cruck was one in which the blades rose to the apex from a tie-beam, around eaves level, the eaves being the lowest part of the roof.

Fig. 8   A mixture of periods.

POST-AND-TRUSS (OR POST-AND-PANEL)

Tie-beams joined pairs of posts at each side of the building. Above the tie-beams were fixed the principal rafters, which were joined by a collar supported by a pair of vertical struts. Each of these supporting units was called a framed truss or tie-beam truss (*see* page 13).

To lend greater structural integrity, diagonal bracing pieces were positioned between the main posts and the wall plates. The wall structure could be lightweight, as it was not required to have any load-bearing function.

BOX-FRAME

Unlike post-and-truss, the roof weight was carried on the framed external side walls, which provided continuous bearing support, consequently removing the need for trusses or purlins. The roof rested on a pair of rafters joined by a collar at their apex.

Box-frames were particularly recognisable because of the many vertical studs the full height of each storey wall. Though not always true, box-frame buildings tended to have tall narrow panels in comparison to post-and-truss, the panels of which tended to be almost square because of the extra horizontal timbering. Sometimes there was ornamental timber-work (quatrefoil) within these panels.

Another way to distinguish between box-frame and post-and-truss is to examine the gable ends (triangular ends of the building): post-and-truss has purlins protruding beyond the gable's face, whereas purlins are not usually present in box-frame construction.

Features common to both the post-and-truss and box-frame include the following:

• Footings – the base structure set into soil on which a building rests. They were built as a plinth using local materials, for example stone or flint, and there was no damp proof course.

11

- Sill-beams (timbers at the base of the building) were positioned on top of this plinth, framed together at an angle to discourage water.
- Studs were set into the sill-beams, and framed into wall plates at the top for a single storey, or into a larger joist for two storeys. Until the mid-sixteenth century, studs could be set at intervals of only their own width (close-studding), but later, to save timber, the panels to be infilled became progressively wider. Therefore, the closer the studs and the larger their scantling, the older the building.
- Until the early sixteenth century, floor joists were heavy beams 200mm (8in) wide by 125mm (5in) deep, laid flat on their sides. As the era progressed their size decreased, as did the size of the studs, which were placed wider apart.

Only in the seventeenth century did carpenters realize that greater tensile strength could be achieved by laying joists on their narrow edges.

ROOF TIMBERS

The pitch is the slope of a roof. The smaller the size of the roofing material, the steeper the pitch needed to be. Thatch and plain tiles required a steep pitch, and each of these materials could follow curves and undulations that larger tiles could not accommodate.

Principal rafters are the structural beams that lie directly underneath the roofing material, sloping accordingly. Single-framed roofs have no purlins, the rafters being braced at various intervals, whilst double-framed roofs have purlins:

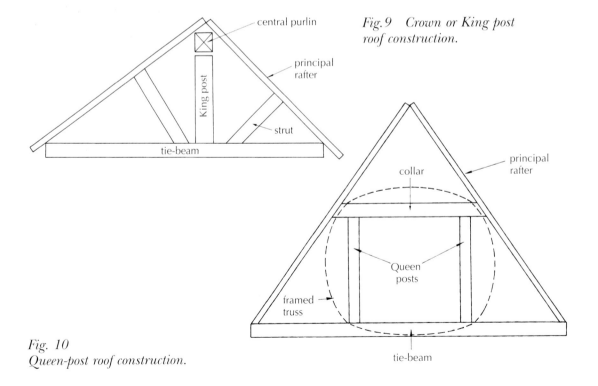

Fig. 9   Crown or King post roof construction.

Fig. 10
Queen-post roof construction.

*Fig. 11   Front view –
gable wall, dormer
windows, tiled
frontage.*

following the same principles as for cruck construction, the purlins were laid across pairs of rafters, at right angles to them.

Crown-post, or King-post, roofs are double-framed, with a large vertical central Crown or King post, a central purlin laid along its top at the ridge, and many rafters joining at, and resting on top of, the central purlin. Other Crown posts were inserted at intervals (sometimes supported by angled struts) to lend support to the central purlin; the base of these Crown posts rested on tie-beams. Horizontal collars would join the pairs of rafters near their apex, giving additional support.

A Queen post roof is comprised of a series of framed trusses. A framed truss is a framework made up of four pieces of timber that collectively support a pair of principal rafters. The bases of the rafters are joined by a horizontal tie-beam, and a horizontal collar joins them near the top. Between the tie-beam and the collar are two vertical Queen posts, supporting the collar near its ends and equidistant from the ends of the tie-beam. Additional struts were sometimes added. Purlins join these trusses, which support the common rafters that are smaller than principal rafters and run parallel to them.

JETTYING

Jettying is where the upper storey projects beyond the lower, and in this instance a beam called a summer supports (carries) the floor joists, and was positioned at the back of the overhang. The floor joist ends were normally shaped into a quarter-circle shape and left exposed. Jettying can occur on one or more sides of a building, and sometimes on all four. Jettied buildings were most popular during the Tudor period, even though the technique had been used in town and country since the late middle ages.

13

Advantages of the Jetty

- Provided extra space in upper-storey rooms.
- Allowed the use of single-storey height posts for buildings of two storeys or more.
- Helped counterbalance upper-storey floor loads. With the floor joists laid flat there was a tendency for them to bow in the centre – the cantilever effect produced by support from the lower wall helped to counteract this.
- Reduced damp problems. The jetty had a shielding effect, preventing rainwater from the roof from being blown back against the walls.
- Appearance. The aesthetically pleasing profile of one or more jetties on a building may have been a stronger motive for such constructions than the other, more practical advantages, since its use never superseded straightforward building techniques.

Techniques of Jettying

If the building was only jettied on one side, the floor joists were simply cantilevered over the lower wall. If two adjacent floors were jettied, it was necessary to alter the direction of the floor joists: one joist was replaced by a larger one, to which a diagonal dragon beam was attached at a 45-degree angle, going into and out of the corner. Floor joists were framed (jointed) into each side of the dragon beam, meeting it at an angle. The other end of the dragon beam was supported by, and fixed to, a huge, often elaborately-carved corner post (a dragon post). A curved bracket attached to the post would support the projecting outer end of the dragon beam. Additional curved bracket supports were also sometimes used along the length of the wall, these being fixed to the lower wall's studs. Sill-beams were laid along the ends of the floor joists, and studs for the upper storey fastened on to these. The same procedure could be followed for a third storey, jettying out over the second.

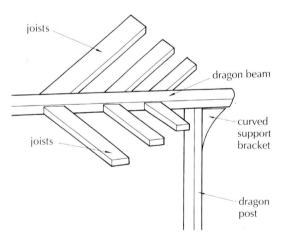

joists

dragon beam

curved support bracket

joists

dragon post

Fig. 12 Jetty construction for two jettied walls meeting at a corner.

GLOSSARY OF TIMBERS

Blades The curved huge timbers attached at the apex in cruck buildings.

Bressumer Similar to the summer, but used on buildings with no jetty. Often decorated with carved leaves or dragons, for example. Also the name given to any heavy timber that spanned an opening as a lintel, for example over a fireplace.

Close-studding Studding set very close together, the gaps equal in width to that of the timber used.

Collar A shorter timber to link vertical or curving timbers (often roof rafters) near their apex to give structural stability.

Joist Heavy piece of timber supporting a floor or ceiling, often an abbreviation of floor joist.

Purlin Longitudinal roof timbers supporting rafters.

Figs 13 and 14   Tudor reproduction – very similar to the real thing.

15

Fig. 15   The old juxtaposed with the new.

Rafters Otherwise known as principal rafters, these were sloping timbers on which roofing materials were fixed. Pairs of common rafters were smaller than principal rafters, and were positioned parallel to them at intervals to lend additional support to a roof.

Rail Timber fixed horizontally.

Ridge beam The horizontally-laid timber along the central apex of a building's roof.

Scantling Smaller pieces of timber used to link larger pieces. Not of large enough cross-section to sustain constructional weights.

Sill-beam Also known as a sole plate or sill plate. Timber laid at the base of a wall.

Stud Timber fixed vertically.

Studding The name given to a series of vertically-placed studs that created a wall panel when the gaps between them were filled.

Summer A large timber joist, on which floor joists rest, on a building with jettying. It is situated at the front of the building, at the back of the overhang.

Tie-beams The horizontally-laid timbers that join either the blades of cruck buildings at their base, or the bases of principal rafters in a roof truss.

Transom Horizontal timber laid across an opening, smaller than a bressumer.

Fig. 16   Copy of Dutch style of building.

16

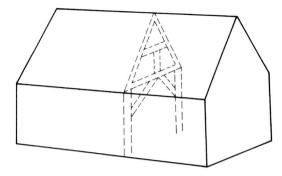

Fig. 17   Ground-floor hall (one storey).

Truss A frame of timbers used to support a roof at various intervals.

Vertical posts Vertically-placed timbers, usually at the corners of a building, on which roof timbering rests.

Wall plate The horizontally-laid timber on which the upper-storey floor joists rest.

LATE MEDIEVAL HALLS

The word 'hall' described a central and important functional area, rather than the utilitarian corridor with stairs we think of today. Many grand houses were nothing but large halls, with private rooms tacked on at each end. The hall element was intrinsic, and was usually included in the house name.

Before medieval times, aisled halls were common – single-storey structures divided into aisles by lines of wooden or stone posts. Late medieval houses, however, were single-spanned, with no aisles. The central hall was one storey, and separated the other two parts of the house at upper-storey level. There were also sizeable first-floor chambers at each end.

The fire in the centre of the hall originally had only a hole in the roof as a chimney, but the development of real chimneys and chimney stacks was followed by floors in these halls, which unified the whole structure.

GROUND-FLOOR HALLS

These single-storey structures were rectangular, with no room divisions. In the basic hall, the roof was carried by the walls, and the floor area was unobstructed. The aisled hall carried the roof on trusses based on stone piers or timber posts running along the length of the wall, which divided the floor space into a central nave with flanking aisles; it had an overhanging roof and the interior had many structural timbers.

Both had an entrance in one of the long sides. They were sometimes divided at the centre, with a central open fire. Some later halls had one end partitioned off from the rest. The earliest of these types of hall were built for the rich, in Suffolk, Essex, Kent and Sussex.

FIRST-FLOOR HALLS

Designed for the upper classes, the principal room of these long buildings was the main, upper-storey hall, which had no ceiling. Adjacent to this was a much

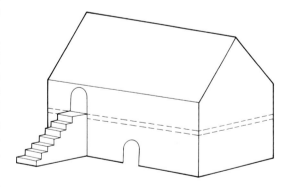

Fig. 18   First-floor hall (two storeys).

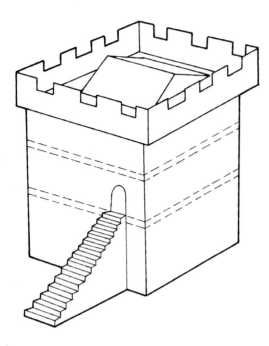

Fig. 19   Tower house (three storeys).

battlements surrounding a pitched or flat roof. Entry to the hall was via an external staircase, with winding staircases leading up to the chambers above, or down to the ground-floor cellar, which was used for storage. They were normally built of stone. Larger tower houses had walls dividing up the space into rooms. They were often built near the curtain walls of a castle.

SINGLE-ENDED (T-SHAPED) HALLS, OR END-HALL HOUSES

This style of hall can be viewed as the forerunner of the large house as we know it today. A single-storey ground-floor hall, in which a 'Lord of the Manor' could perform public duties, was joined at right angles to a two-storey domestic end block, intended for private use. The hall may or may not have been aisled, and there was usually a central open hearth or a fireplace along the rear-side wall.

The domestic end block was like a first-floor hall or solar, without a ceiling, and

smaller, ceilinged room. Underneath this the inferior ground floor area (undercroft) was either undivided or divided to correspond with the rooms above. The upper and ground floors were totally separate, with different entrances, entry to the upper floor hall being via an external staircase.

There was a side wall fireplace for the hall above, but not usually any heating for the ground floor. The main hall was used as a public room, with the smaller upstairs room intended for domestic purposes. The ground floor was either occupied by a social inferior, or used for storage.

TOWER HOUSES

A tower house was the name given to a first-floor hall raised over an undercroft, with one or two storeys (usually single rooms) above this, and terminating in

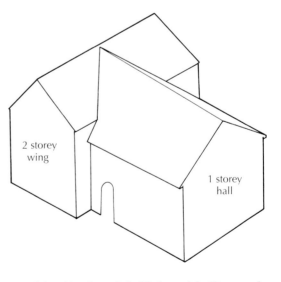

2 storey wing

1 storey hall

Fig. 20   Single-ended (T-shaped hall) or end-hall house.

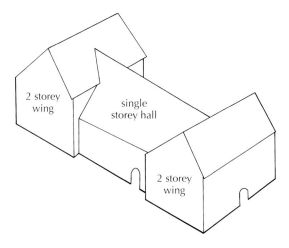

Fig. 21 Double-ended hall.

above one or more rooms. The upper room may or may not have had a fireplace, but the lower rooms were without provision for heating. Earlier halls were accessed via an external staircase, and there was no communication between the upper and lower rooms or between the upper rooms and the hall.

Construction was either timber-framed or stone, but a combination of stone wing and timber-framed hall was common. In the latter case stone could be used for extra storeys, when height and stability was needed and the size of roof and floor-beams was of less importance; timber framing for the hall reflected the requirement for width and height. The stone block at the end offered a greater measure of protection than timber, should the need for defence arise.

Existing halls of this type have usually had an intermediate floor added.

DOUBLE-ENDED (H-SHAPED) HALLS

This structure comprised a central hall, with cross wings set at right angles at each end. As with single-ended halls, the central hall was for public occasions, whilst the two-storey accommodation on either side was for domestic use; each wing could function as an independent unit. The entrance was at the junction between the lower end of the hall and one of the cross wings.

The central hall was used as a courtroom or council chamber, with a public entrance and assembly space at one end, an unobstructed main area, and a raised platformed area known as a dais at the other end, with rooms leading off it. The lower part of the hall was for the general populace, while the dais area was for the presiding dignitaries. The lower end had front and back doors, doors to the buttery, pantry, kitchen and staircase, and two openings which led to the main part of the hall. There was an inner porch, protecting the hall from the worst draughts, used as an anteroom when the hall was used as courtroom, and a servery when it was used for banquets.

The dais was intended for the higher ranks, who were protected from down draughts by a covered canopy of timber or

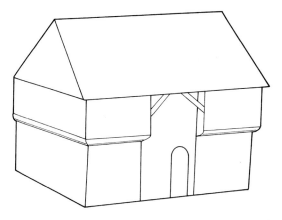

Fig. 22 Wealden house – jettied at the front and at both ends, with a unified, hipped roof.

19

plaster. There was also a bay window and doors at each end to allow access to the upper parts of the cross wings of the house.

The wings contained a buttery, pantry, plus a solar or great chamber at one end, with drawing rooms and another chamber at the other. All rooms apart from the service sections had fireplaces and were generally much more comfortable than the hall. Separate staircases at each end allowed direct access to most of the rooms.

THE WEALDEN HOUSE

This was an extremely attractive, typically Tudor house, characteristically with a jetty at the front and sides. The end sections corresponded with the end wings of the double-ended halls, from which they evolved, the major difference being that the Wealden had a single-hipped or gablet roof (*see* Chapter 2), thereby unifying the whole structure. The jetty was either at the front and sides, as stated, completely absent, just at the front, or to the front, sides and rear. A common feature was particularly close vertical studding, and the use of bulky decorated timbers both for external timber-work and the roof trusses.

It was a type of open-hall house, where the main room was a single-storey hall at ground level (with no ceiling), with two-storey sections at one or both ends. The entrance was through a cross-passage (cross-entry) to one end of the hall,

Fig. 23   Single-storey.

20

therefore just to the right or left of one of the end sections. When the Wealden had two-storeys at both ends, there were service rooms to one side of the entry, and, at the other end, doors leading to one or more parlours, above which were one or more chambers.

A sectional bird's eye plan would show a rectangle at ground-floor level, an H-shape at first-floor level (if front jetties were present) and a rectangle at roof level; the overall roof simply covered the set-back central (hall) section with deep eaves. Although resembling a double-ended hall, the ends did not project as wings as in the familiar H-shaped double-ended hall pattern, and the house was much smaller.

The Wealden was first developed in the mid-fourteenth century, was still being built in the mid-sixteenth century, and was therefore contemporary with most of the Tudor period. It was normally occupied by yeomen farmers rather than gentlemen.

Present-day Wealdens have often been modernised during the second half of the sixteenth century, by the insertion of an intermediate floor in the hall, establishing a great chamber with a large dormer window. There is usually a hearth, fireback wall and chimney-hood behind the cross-passage, or a fireplace within or against the cross-passage. First-floor chambers in the wings are reached by separate stairs within each.

2

Exterior Features

INFILLING

This was the process of filling the spaces between the upright vertical timber studding with a walling material.

WATTLE AND DAUB

This was the most popular method of infilling. Wattle was made up of vertical staves of hazel, cleft chestnut or oak that were sprung between holes in the upper rails (horizontal timbers) and grooves or holes in the lower rail, about 250mm (10in) to 300mm (12in) apart. Wands of pliable hazel or ash were woven horizontally between these, but were not needed for panels of close-studding, as used in the early part of the Tudor period. For long panels, a short cross-piece might have been sprung between studs, while the staves were tied. As an alternative, horizontal sticks might have been used, wedged between the studs in the same manner as the staves were wedged vertically.

Daub was wet clay or mud mixed with chopped straw or cow hair and cow dung, sometimes with lime added. The daub was forcefully thrown from both sides simultaneously to fill the holes in the framework of sticks. Successive layers were subsequently applied, and covered with a thin plaster coat, made from lime, sand and cow hair, before a coat of limewash was applied.

Wattle and daub is still used for repairs to old houses, and the original material, taken from demolished buildings, can be reconstituted by specialist techniques before being used again.

BRICK NOGGING

Infilling panels with bricks was a process that began in the seventeenth century, after the Tudor period. But since it was

Fig. 24   Herringbone-style brick nogging between timber framing.

English bond   herringbone

Figs. 25 and 26   Two types of brick nogging.

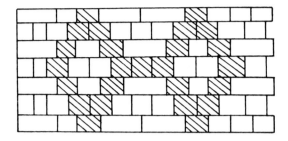

Fig. 27   Diapering pattern in brick.

often used on Tudor buildings, usually as a method of repairing damaged wattle and daub, it is as relevant to Tudor dolls' houses as any other kind of modernization that remains in sympathy with the building. The straightforward 'stretcher-bond' style of infilling was not especially attractive, but the herringbone style was extremely impressive. Unfortunately, since the timbers were not designed to support the weight of bricks, structural problems with the timber frame could occur. The brick, being more porous than the wattle

and daub, could also allow the ingress of damp. Luckily both problems are irrelevant to dolls' house construction.

A diaper was a pattern of diamonds, squares or lozenge shapes created by using bricks of two colours.

COLOURS

The archetypal black-and-white Tudor house is historically inaccurate, since no permanent black colour was available until the nineteenth century. But does it really matter if the original untreated oak timber weathered to a silvery colour, and the wattle and daub panels were finished in a dull yellow or red earth-based wash? Black beams and white panels can look attractive and are evocative of the era, and if the paint technology had been available the builders might easily have chosen these colours themselves.

Panels and beams can be virtually any colour. Yellow panelling against dark

Fig. 28   Close-up of brick nogging.

23

brown timber can be extremely attractive, exemplified by some houses in Lavenham, Suffolk. Light blue or pink panels against black timbers are also possibilities. You may have come across other equally attractive contrasting colours on timber-framed buildings, which could in turn look wonderful on a dolls' house.

CLADDING

For practical reasons of weatherproofing, timber-framed houses were often clad all over by external plastering, completely concealing the timber and panels. The unrelieved monotony of such a finish was sometimes relieved by decorative effects such as pargeting.

Pargeting

Originally a term used to denote any type of plaster sheathing, it has now come to mean ornamental external plaster-work, either incised or raised. Incised pargeting was typically stick-work or combed-work, where single sticks or groups of sticks were used to scratch a design into the wet material to effect a result similar to textured finish stippling-type decorations used on ceilings today. Normally the wall was divided into conveniently-sized bordered panels within which a design – typically fans, herringbones or scallops – was scribed. Pargeting can look especially eye-catching when picked out in such colours as pink, yellow and blue.

Fig. 29   Two types of pargeting pattern.

Raised pargeting took the form of decorative swags, foliage, crowns and suns, for example.

WEATHERBOARDING (CLAPBOARDING)

This was used predominantly on smaller buildings such as cottages, farm buildings and windmills. Weatherboarding is thought to have begun in around 1600, but was not considered really popular until the eighteenth century. Originally, untreated oak or elm was pegged to the frame, but later softwood panels were nailed horizontally to the studs, each piece overlapping the one below. It was feather-edged, the thicker edge below and the thinner overlapped by the one above, in a similar pattern to modern featherboarded fencing styles, except that it was horizontal rather than vertical. Often painted white or cream, weatherboarded properties proliferated in the Weald of Kent, giving rise to the name 'Kent weatherboarding'.

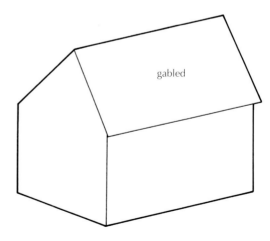

Fig. 30   Different kinds of roof (above and facing page).

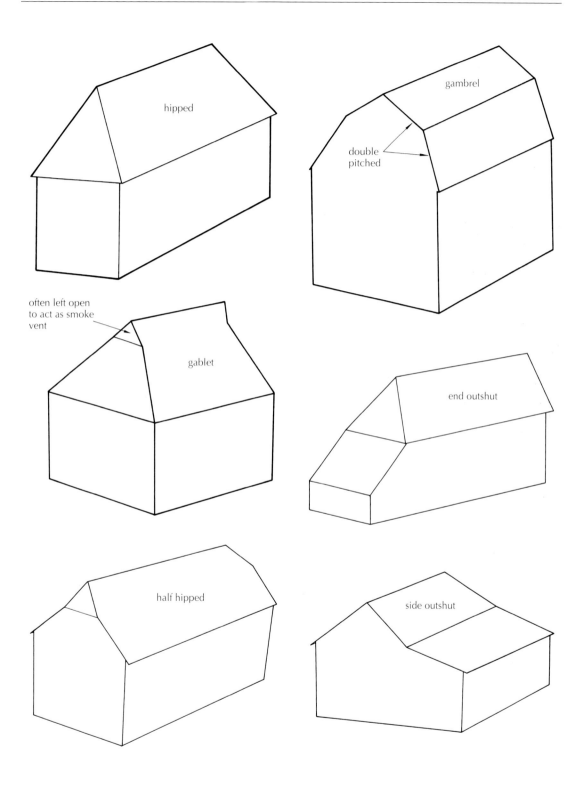

hipped

gambrel

double
pitched

often left open
to act as smoke
vent

gablet

end outshut

half hipped

side outshut

Fig. 31   Exceptionally steep tiled roof.

ROOFS

The roof was an integral part of the timber frame of cruck properties, whereas in post-and-truss or box-frame buildings the roof was separate, reliant on the strength of the walls for support. There are three factors to be considered: the type of roof and roofing material and method of roof construction.

TYPES OF ROOF

Hipped Sloping on all four sides.

Gabled Two sloping sides meeting at a long ridge at the apex. The roof rests on the side (gable) walls of the house, the upper part of which is 'V'-shaped accordingly.

Variations

Gambrel A gabled roof, with two angles of slope in order to allow maximum headroom.

Half-hipped A cross between a hipped and gabled roof: the 'V' of the side walls changes to a slope near the roof's apex.

Gablet A hipped roof, with the final upper part of two of the narrower sloped sides changing to a vertical direction. Before chimney stacks were invented, these top sections could be left open to act as a smoke vent.

End outshut or catslide The main slope of the roof continued down at an altered angle to cover a single-storey room at the end of the house.

Side outshut or catslide As above, with the extra room located at the side of the house.

ROOFING MATERIALS

Thatch

Thatch is the oldest roofing material known, and is made up of bundles of reeds, straw or heather. It requires a steep pitch, and can be swept around angles, thus enabling it to be used to create curving slopes above windows known as 'eyebrows'.

In the Tudor period, the most commonly-used material was straw. The process, called yealming, involved wetting the straw by soaking, then forming it into bundles called yealms.

The four methods of applying the yealms to the roof were as follows.

(1) Pinning it down using a system of rods or sways.
(2) Sewing it to the rafters. This method is commonly used today, often in combination with the rod system.
(3) Working the material into layers of turf. The turf layers were spread across the timber rafters, then the yealms were secured into the earth's surface by extracting a length of straw (a staple) from the top of each yealm and working these into the turf.
(4) Keeping them in place by means of a covering of weighted ropes, though this method was rarely used.

Long-Straw Thatch

Beginning at the eaves (lowest part) of the roof, the yealms were laid in place, then tied or held down by hazel rods secured to the rafter by nailed-in hooks (called spars nowadays, but previously known as broaches, spears, sparrows, bucklers or pricks). Subsequent layers of yealms were laid on top, overlapping those below by two-thirds. At the ridge (apex) of the roof, yealms were placed on top of and at right angles to the rest, then fixed securely. Finally, the cap was fashioned on the ridge by bending yealms centrally across the ridge, folding half down either side. It was held in place by sways stapled down on top, known as liggers. Liggers were added on top of other parts of the roof that may have been vulnerable to the wind, notably the eaves, and the replication of these liggers can lend additional authenticity to a dolls' house. The edges are then trimmed and the thatching combed through.

Particularly attractive areas of thatching were at the ridge, where caps could be trimmed at their base edge in zigzags or scallop shapes, the liggers above sometimes arranged as two parallel lines with liggers fixed in between to form a pattern.

Stone slates

These are otherwise known as slate stones, stone tiles or tilestones.

Limestone Cotswold slates 13mm (½in) to 38mm (1½in) thick, and creamy yellow, weathering to yellow/brown.
Purbeck stone Heavy, 19mm (¾in) thick, shades of grey, blue-grey and brown.
Collyweston slates Light, 9mm (⅜in) thick, cream and grey.

Sandstone Also called flags, for example Millstone Grit. These tiles are much larger

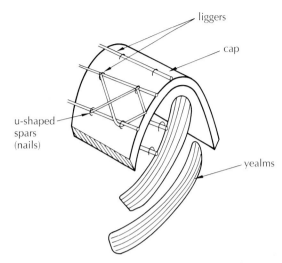

Fig. 32 Thatching detail at ridge of roof.

and heavier than limestone, up to 75mm (3in) thick.

Holes were punched into the slates either in the centre of the top upper edge, or at each side of the top edge. Beginning at the eaves, tiles were nailed in place on to laths, which were nailed at right angles to the rafters, succeeding rows of slates overlapping those below (they were nailed with oak pegs). The joints were arranged so that they were staggered, with a double row at the eaves, the lower of which were referred to as 'soakers'.

The courses were widest at the eaves, becoming gradually smaller up the roof to the narrowest at the ridge. Ridges were often covered with freestone, with a 'V'-shape carved from underneath.

'True' Slate

True slate is much thinner and lighter than stone slate, and until the advent of the railways only local sources were used, as follows:

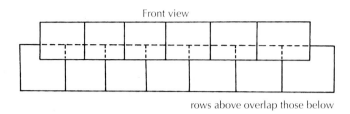

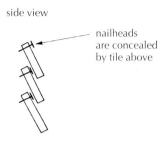

nailheads are concealed by tile above

Figs. 33 and 34   Method of fitting roof slates or tiles.

- Scotland – dark blue to mid-blue.
- Wales – blue, blue-purple and grey, blue-grey.
- Cornwall and Devon – grey, weathering to grey-green and red. Small Cornish slates were known as 'peggies'.
- Cumbria – light green, olive, silver and grey-green, pale green, green, blue-black and blue-grey.
- Leicestershire – uncharacteristically thick and heavy for true slate, between 13mm (½in) to 19mm (¾in) thick. Blue-grey.

Plain Tiles

These were manufactured by firing clay, just as bricks were made. The size was standardized in 1477, and is still the same today: 267mm (10½in) × 158mm (6¼in) × 16mm (⅝in). They were pointed underneath with lime hair mortar to weatherproof them, a process called 'torching'. For the ridge, half-round or saddle-back tiles were used, and saddle-back and bonnet tiles were used for hip junctions.

As with bricks, colours of clay varied across the country. Most, however, were various shades of red.

CHIMNEY STACKS AND CHIMNEYS

As well as smoke from the fire escaping from a central hole in the roof and from the windows, some larger properties had gablet roofs, with specially-made holes between the ridge and hip, known as smoke gablets, allowing a more efficient exit.

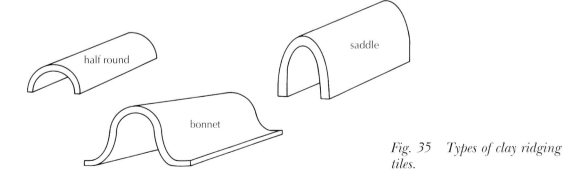

Fig. 35   Types of clay ridging tiles.

Early chimney stacks and chimneys were simply a makeshift arrangement of timbers covered with wattle and daub, and perhaps plastered inside. Thatched homes continued the thatching around the chimney itself. In towns, as soon as brick and stone alternatives were possible, this quickly became the norm from the fifteenth century onwards. In fact, for safety reasons, legislation was introduced in the fourteenth century stating that chimneys must be built of brick, plaster or stone, rather than timber. Brick, rather than stone, tended to be the more popular material for stacks and chimneys.

First of all, stacks were built as a separate outcrop on to an outside (gable/side) wall, but later the axial stack grew in popularity, and was positioned in the centre of the building between the parlour and the hall. The advantage was that the central stack could be shared by fireplaces in each of the downstairs rooms, and sometimes fireplaces in the chambers above. The conventional 'outside wall' stack was still in use, however, in many timber-framed homes. A third alternative was to build the stack on the inside of the gable wall, rather than the outside. The stack was sometimes even positioned on the front wall (notably in Devon), but this was more as a matter of convenience than for any aesthetic reason.

Wealthy farmers and merchants regarded chimneys as a vehicle with which to display their status, leading to Tudor

Fig. 36   Oriel window in a gable wall.

chimneys becoming recognisable by their fine moulded brickwork. Brick chimneys on large sixteenth-century houses were often tall, elaborate, and hexagonal, octagonal, spiral, fluted, rectangular or square shapes. Since bricks were available in many colours – reds, oranges, blues, purples, browns and blacks – sometimes the different colours were juxtaposed to create an attractive effect. Some smaller homes had equally impressive chimneys. A typical late Tudor/early Elizabethan chimney is likely to appear as a cluster of angled shafts, some decorated and some plain; however several of these were likely to be purely for show, with only one or two having functioning flues.

WINDOWS

In early Tudor times only grand houses or ecclesiastical buildings had their windows glazed, because glass was expensive. Window openings, known as lights, were set very high up, usually just under the eaves, and would have had shutters inside or been covered with vellum, cloth or paper; lattices of wood, reed or wickerwork were also used, the lattices formed into diamond shapes, and the framed assembly called a fenestral. Vertical timber or stone mullions served not only to divide the area for additional security, but also supported the lintel, or bressumer, above. As a rule, the square-section timber or

Fig. 37   Large glazed opening below jetty.

stone mullions were not set squarely, but rotated through 45 degrees (set diagonally), so that their long corner edges were frontwards, thus maximizing the space available for the entry of light. The reveals or jambs – the stone, brick or timber structures at the sides of the window opening – were also often diagonally angled in this way for the same reason. But when oiled cloth was used as a window covering the mullions were usually set squarely, in order to accommodate the panel upright.

Non-opening timber-framed windows, surrounding an iron frame for leaded-light units, were incorporated into homes from the late sixteenth century, and mullion and transom windows (transoms being horizontal bars serving to strengthen the units) began to proliferate as glass became more generally available. Tudor arches were formed above, and the frames were decorated with tracery. Rainhoods were structures of projecting brickwork above the windows, protecting them from the weather. Opening casement windows were invented latterly; these consisted of iron or wood frames encasing the glass panels, hinged at one side and with decorative iron catches and stays.

Oriel windows were set into a structure that was stepped out from the front of the building, as a kind of separate box. These were usually three-sided boxes, with corner angles of 90 degrees or wider. The structure was supported by elaborately-carved corbels (supporting pieces set underneath, at right angles to the wall) or carved figures built out at an angle, or else the underside of the oriel's outcrop formed a smooth curve. Bow windows curved, and whilst they were not used in Tudor times, they could easily have been added at a later date. Dormer windows were built into the slope of the roof, with a section of roof above a triangular window façade, within which was a square or rectangular window. These were first used when open-hall houses were converted into two-storey buildings in the sixteenth century. Bay windows – a three-sided glazed extension to a room – were first used in Elizabethan days, but only on the most stylish houses.

SHUTTERS

Internal or external timber shutters were used on cottages for security and weatherproofing, either instead of, or in addition to, conventional windows. They were hinged on the side, top or bottom. If they were hinged at the top they were kept open by a hook from a ceiling-beam if internal, or by a pole if external. Alternatively, cottage shutters sometimes slid into position horizontally.

GLASS

In 1567 Elizabeth I allowed *gentilshommes verriers* from Lorraine to manufacture window glass in England. These 'gentleman glassmakers' made broad glass, produced from a treacly heated mixture of sand, soda and lime by a method known as the broad glass process. A blowpipe was inserted into the molten material and a glass cylinder blown by mouth, then stretched into a sausage shape, cut open and flattened out. The sheets were of limited size, slightly wavy and uneven, and tended to discolour quickly. Usually they were cut to a diamond or lozenge shape, roundels of stained glass being something of a speciality for opulent buildings only. Sixteenth- and seventeenth-century glass is sometimes slightly tinted, is frequently pale yellow because of impurities in the manufacturing sand, and also contains bubbles known as seeds.

LEADED LIGHTS

Only small pieces of glass could be produced, therefore larger panels were made by joining these pieces into a unified whole by means of strips of lead, forming leaded lights. Small panes (quarries) were held together by specially produced lead cames – strips of lead of an H-shaped cross-section. The quarries, diamond- or rectangular-shaped, were inserted each side of the central bar of the 'H' shape, with cement (linseed putty) holding them in place. The cames were then soldered together from the outside to make a uniform whole. After positioning in a window opening, they would be reinforced with a horizontal iron saddle bar on the inside.

GLOSSARY OF WINDOW TERMS

Came A lead strip of H-shaped cross-section used to hold quarries together in the production of leaded lights.

Casement windows Iron- or wood-framed windows that open at the side.

Fenestral The framed wooden assembly used to support oiled-cloth window coverings.

Mullion and transom A type of window with mullions and transoms dividing the area horizontally and vertically.

Mullions Timber or stone upright bars that divide a window area vertically.

Quarries Small panes of glass used to make leaded lights.

Rainhoods Projecting brickwork above windows, protecting them from the weather.

Reveals or jambs The sides of the window opening in the building wall.

Seeds Bubbles apparent in old glass.

3

Interior Features

HISTORICALLY ACCURATE INTERIORS?

Most people's image of the ideal Tudor house interior will probably be something of a mish-mash, with extra floors, higher ceilings, and external staircases and central fireplaces removed. This is hardly surprising, as few unadulterated examples now remain. In fact this familiar, less spartan interior is much more attractive, appealing and comfortable than the genuine article, yet it still retains an essentially 'Tudor' quality.

Painstakingly recreating the stark interiors of the sixteenth century might seem unrewarding, and would have minimal play value for a child. A good compromise is to replicate the major structural Tudor features, such as ceiling-beams, inglenook fireplaces and spiral staircases, but to incorporate the likely seventeenth-century alterations, by adding an intermediate floor in the hall section of a house and making extra rooms, for example. Similarly, external stone staircases are not likely to appeal to twentieth-century ideas of luxury, and no one would envisage a present-day family storing grain and farm produce in the whole of the downstairs section of a domestic home, as our farming ancestors did.

Some may wish to aim for absolute historical accuracy when creating a dolls' house interior, whilst others may prefer the mish-mash approach outlined above.

Whichever style interests you, it will be helpful to have an understanding of the original interiors, if only to decide how best to adapt them.

ROOMS

The concept of a home being used simply for sleeping, eating and relaxing is relatively modern. In the Tudor period, work and domesticity were irrevocably intertwined, but one facet of the growing prosperity of the times was that less of the home needed to be used for business, and more areas could be devoted to domestic activities. In practical terms, this meant the division of larger rooms into smaller ones and the introduction of extra furniture.

GROUND FLOOR

Living Room
Also known as a hall, bodystead, or house-stead. The living room was the most important room, and sometimes the only one with a fireplace. As well as being the family's main room for relaxing and entertaining, it was used for, amongst other things, cooking, and contained a beam from which to hang pots over the fire (a reckan), plus all the requisite fire tools. Furniture might have included a trestle table, chairs, forms (long benches without backs), and a cabinet or shelves to house crockery.

Parlour

Also known as a chamber or bower.

A private room for sleeping, containing bed(s), chairs and cupboards, the parlour was also sometimes used for the storage of goods. As the trend for sleeping upstairs increased, the parlour became a dining room, with a table, chairs and a fireplace for warmth (not for cooking).

Pantry

The pantry was a store room for dry foodstuffs, and could sometimes simply be a space divided off from the parlour.

Larder

The larder was similar to the pantry, used for the storage of meat.

Buttery

Also known as a spence or drink-house.

Serving a similar purpose to the pantry, the cool conditions of the buttery were specifically conducive to the storage of food items in barrels and tubs.

Kitchen

Originally detached from the main house, the kitchen was not incorporated into the structure until much later, when cooking was done here rather than in the living room. It would contain the usual cooking equipment. When making a dolls' house, most people dislike using the living room as a kitchen, so a likely compromise would be to adapt one of the parlours.

Service Room

Also known as a low end or back-house.

The service room was at the rear of the house, and was used for the storage of produce and farming equipment.

Outshot

Also known as lean-to or outshut.

A type of service room at the back of the house, the outshot was covered by an extension of the main roof (catslide roof).

Dairy

The dairy was used for storing milk and making cream and butter. It was either in the main house, or a separate structure.

FIRST FLOOR

Bedroom

Also known as a bed chamber, chamber or solar.

Bedrooms sometimes doubled as dry storage areas.

Loft

The loft was a room within the roof space for an unceilinged first floor area.

SECOND (HIGHEST) FLOOR

Garret

Also known as a cockloft or loft.

Similar to the loft, the garret was used either for storage, as an 'apple' loft for example, or as a bedroom for children and/or servants.

FLOORING

Ground floors were initially made of beaten earth, strewn with rushes and straw, and it was not until the seventeenth century that bricks and stone (flagstones) were used, if these materials were locally available. Boarded ground floors date from the beginning of the eighteenth century for larger houses, and a century later for smaller ones.

FLOORBOARDS

These were usually found on upper floors, and often inserted as intermediate floors in a single storey hall. Oak or elm was used, and the planks were at least 305mm (12in) wide, sometimes of uneven width and thickness.

The three main methods of construction were as follows:

(1) Joist-and-boarded. Boards ran parallel with the joists beneath, which were rebated to accept the corners of the boards and were thus part of the floor themselves.
(2) Close-boarded/parallel to joists. Parallel-running boards were pegged to the joists underneath, which were arranged so as to bridge the junctions.
(3) Close-boarded/running across joists. The joists were set wider apart. It was possible to use varying widths of board, and the method is still in use today. Boards can be butt-jointed over a joist without any consequent loss of strength.

Floorboards were produced either by splitting the tree using a special iron tool, or by sawing the trunk with a pit saw. When riven, the boards were of uneven thickness and had to be laid and trimmed with an adze to unify the thickness. At first the trunk was quartered before splitting or sawing, but better boards were later produced by pit-sawing the complete trunk, thereby forming wildly differing widths, many of which were tree-girth width, or close to it.

The underside of the floorboards would often provide the ceiling for the downstairs room, and were sometimes plastered and whitened; reeds were occasionally laid underneath the floor joists to provide a surface on to which the plaster could grip.

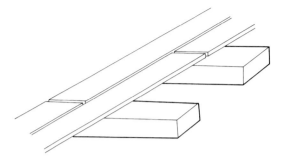

close-boarded at right angles to joist

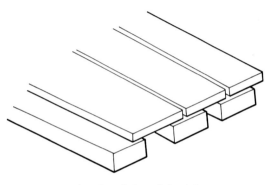

close-boarded parallel to joists

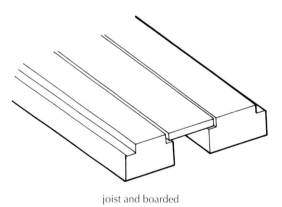

joist and boarded

Fig. 38   Three different methods of floorboarding.

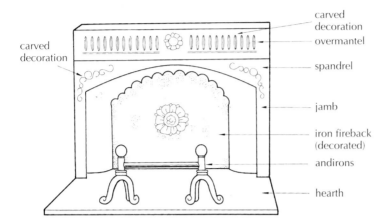

carved
decoration

carved
decoration
overmantel

spandrel

jamb

iron fireback
(decorated)

andirons

hearth

*Fig. 39   Stone fireplace
showing component parts.*

FIREPLACES

The symbolic and practical importance of the fire is perfectly understandable, when its dual role as heater and cooker is considered. In a Tudor dwelling the fire wasn't an inconspicuous convenience, but something to be proud of, to be viewed as the heart of the house. In a timber-framed building the fireplace was often housed within an inglenook – a partitioned-off area of the living room. In a large stone-

or brick-built stately home or castle there would be a stone fireplace with a carved overmantel above, jambs (vertically) either side, and the fire area itself sited on a hearth within a brick-lined recess in the wall.

INGLENOOK FIREPLACES

The inglenook (meaning chimney corner) was a definite improvement on the living room's central fire, whose chimney was a

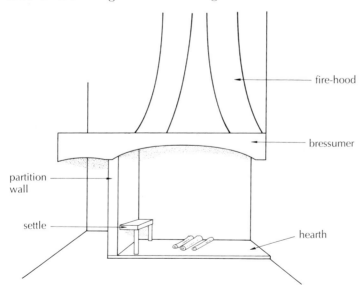

fire-hood

bressumer

partition
wall

settle

hearth

*Fig. 40   Inglenook fireplace
arrangement in a living room.*

Fig. 41   Fireplace showing bressumer and chimney piece within cavity.

smoke bay in the roof. The idea of smoke and fire being created at one side of the room might have seemed wasteful until people realised that heat could travel laterally, across the room.

Early inglenooks took up a large area of the living room. They were bounded on two sides by the house walls, one of which might be an interior wall. The third side was a partition within the room, surmounted at its front by a large timber joist called a bressumer. A fixed settle or bench was positioned against this partition wall. The fire was made on a built-up hearthstone (flagstones or slate), and above it was a cylindrical brick fire-hood (known as a beehive because of its shape), that led up to the chimney. Earlier fire-hoods were made up with wattle and daub.

The bressumer, or lintel, might be elaborately carved and decorated with heraldic badges and mottoes in fine houses, but in humbler dwellings it was usually left plain. In the seventeenth century, recesses in the inglenook's brick walls were created to make cupboards (keeping holes), and also clay 'bread oven' holes that could act as rudimentary ovens. A chain for cooking pots and cauldrons was slung from a beam across the fire-hood opening.

Nowadays, alterations to the original Tudor interiors often mean that the bressumer wall is built right along to the end of the room, making the settle wall look as if it is within the wall of the house itself, particularly when the area surrounding the fire-hood is also covered by a wall. An open fire is now hardly ever made on the original hearth, but on a newer, smaller fireplace and fire-hood built within the old. Fires built in the old way would be likely to fill the room with smoke.

The separate parts of the fireplace include:

- a horizontal mantel, mantelpiece, fire surround, bresummer or lintel, made of wood or stone. Stone mantels were also referred to as the frieze (or lintel), and were often carved with decorations
- vertical jambs
- the hearth. Often slabs of stone or a layer of bricks, this was the fireproof area beneath and directly in front of the fireplace
- the burner unit. Tudor homes would normally have a pair of fire-dogs (andirons) to support large logs, or else an iron box (grate) to contain the kindling
- the fireback. Often made of iron, it might have been embellished with a family crest or other design
- the throat. The inside cavity of the fireplace; the open area beneath the actual chimney.

IRON-WORK

Cast-iron firebacks were often used, sometimes decorated in relief with, for example, a coat of arms. The timber to be burnt was placed on a pair of iron fire-dogs (andirons) to prevent logs from rolling on to the hearth, and these andirons were originally joined by a bar at their base. An adjustable-height crane was used to hang cooking pots above the flames, as well as large andirons connected by a rotatable spit for roasting joints of meat.

WALLS

PLASTER-WORK

Plastering was introduced as a way of smoothing and strengthening wattle and daub surfaces. Wall painting was practised in the mid-sixteenth century and some still survives, occasionally rediscovered after centuries of burial under layers of paint or panelling. Inventive murals, as well as plain colours, were used, and sections of timber panelling were sometimes picked out in different colours too.

Larger houses had decorative friezes depicting various scenes, and towards the end of the Tudor period pargeting (designs in raised plaster) became more popular for interior friezes, with many inventive designs and patterns.

TIMBER PANELLING OR WAINSCOTING

This constituted either an actual partition wall itself, or was applied over a wall, normally in a room of importance. Usually the

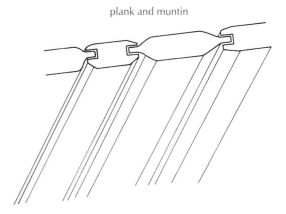

plank and muntin

Fig. 42 Plank and muntin wall panelling.

panelling sections were set on to a sill at the base and had a carved frieze or beam at the top. Originally the oak used was of a light honey colour, but present-day examples have been darkened by age. Sometimes seats and benches were built into the panelling itself.

Plank and Muntin Panelling

These partitions consisted of alternate thick and thin panels of wood, or vertical studs with panels in between, and no horizontal divisions. In early types, the vertical muntins (studding) were split in half and bonded to both sides of the panel to create the raised sections, but later the studs were grooved, and the panels chamfered so as to fit into these This chamfering extended to the panel's face and was echoed on the stud, giving a pleasing effect of raised surfaces, and sometimes the centre of the panels would be carved to give a moulded rib.

Raised Field Panelling

This was made in the same way as plank and muntin, but the panels were much larger than the studs, and there was also horizontal timber framing, creating a series of square or rectangular panels, which were sometimes carved.

Linenfold Panelling (Wavy Woodwork)

This form of panelling consisted of square or rectangular panels, carved to resemble folded cloth. Occasionally carvings were even more intricate, with the addition of flower and fruit motifs. Sometimes, as well as decorations on the frieze above, there were carved pilasters (vertical posts) added at various intervals.

STAIRCASES

Early staircases tended to be concealed and jammed into a tight space, whereas later ones were larger and generally more upfront and confident-looking – the forerunners of proud, welcoming majestic sweeping stairways. A popular location for a staircase was beside a fireplace, going up beside the chimney stack, another being along the rear wall, where the building could be conveniently extended to accommodate it.

After straight ladders with rungs, there was another form of straight staircase, where triangular sections of timber were carried on stretchers to form a rudimentary staircase. The spiral (winding) staircase was more complex, with stone or timber steps set into the wall, the other ends of these curving around a central

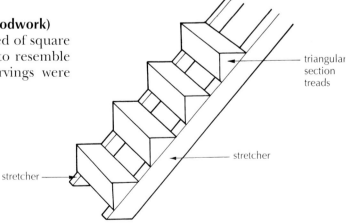

triangular section treads

stretcher

stretcher

Fig. 43   Three types of staircase (continued overleaf).

39

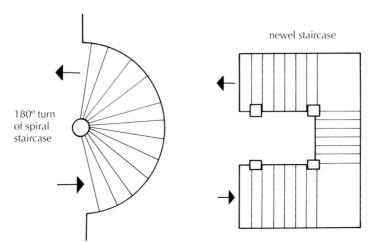

Fig. 43 (continued)

post, called a newel post. Then came the newel staircase, where the steps were fixed at right angles around a newel post. Newel posts were large and carved, and there would be a strong, sometimes elaborately carved balustrade with a broad moulded handrail, rather than separate balusters. The dogleg staircase was invented in the mid-seventeenth century, and this allowed a 180-degree turn instead of 90 degrees. Although outside the Tudor period, a dogleg staircase could legitimately be included in a Tudor dolls' house design, as it could have been installed at the same time as an intermediate floor was put in, in the seventeenth century.

CEILINGS

The ceiling of a room was often the underside of the floorboards of the room above. Later, the underside of the timber was plastered over between the large timber joists. The floor joists often rested on one or more much larger timber beams, set at right angles, to which they were joined. The beams and joists were sometimes decorated by chamfering the edges or carving mouldings and ribs into them. The carved work was also painted.

The chamfer would run along the length of the beam, terminating shortly

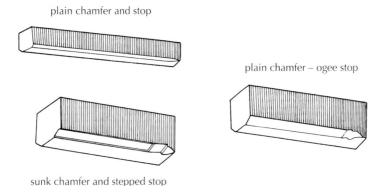

Fig. 44 Different kinds of chamfering on ceiling beams.

Fig. 45   Timber panelling adjoining ceiling.

Fig. 46   Timber panelling on interior walls.

before the end, where it met a wall, the final section called a 'stop'. This stop formed a triangular section, from the corner of the beam to the beginning of the chamfered edge. Alternatively, a plain chamfer might have had an ogee stop; a sunk chamfer was inset from the edge at both sides, and was usually accompanied by a stepped stop.

As with wall panelling, the original ceiling joists and beams were light coloured (untreated), and the now-familiar black-beam white-plaster ceiling was created by the Victorians, who stained the beams black. They might originally have been limewashed, but this would have been with a light colour. Again there is the paradox for a dolls' house constructor: should the joists be left plain, the colour to which a purist house-restorer would try to restore beams, or painted black in the style familiar to everyone?

Alternatively, the timber beams could also be plastered over, and in large houses these plastered ceilings might be decorated. The areas were originally divided into rectangular or square sections by creating moulded ribs (to give an effect similar to plain timber wall panelling). Later, the dividing ribs gave way to strap-work, including various shapes, scrolls, figures and other elaborate decorations, with Elizabethan ceilings featuring fine geometric designs. In more humble dwellings, the ceiling plaster-work was left plain.

Wooden friezes were carved to match the beams, whereas plastered ceilings had matching plaster friezes. Friezes were more popular than decorative covings, and were more highly decorated than the ceilings, with a huge variety of topical designs.

DOORS

In some ways, medieval doors on stone buildings looked similar to church doors, in that they were made of heavy nail-studded oak, arching to a point at the top and set into a bulky frame or hung directly on the wall with an iron pin. They were bulky, unwelcoming and crude. Sixteenth-century doors became less pointed, and on timber-framed buildings were usually squared, but the woodworkers' lack of finesse was still apparent, and it was not until the seventeenth century that doors became less gauche.

Very early doors were short and thick-set, hung directly to the walls with large

Fig. 47   Typical timber door.

iron pins, or surrounded by solid timber frames. Exterior doors often had a stone or brick course above them, known as a label – this outcrop prevented water from running on to the door. Interior doors did not have architraves (timber door surrounds), that became usual in subsequent periods.

BATTEN DOOR

The batten door was made up of vertical oak planks butted together and bonded at the back to horizontal battens or ledges (usually four), with clenched wrought iron nails or wooden pegs. Diagonal braces were sometimes added between the battens to consolidate the structure. The modern equivalent is called a framed and braced door. Broader planks were sometimes grooved to give a narrower appearance and the vertical joins were protected by thin oak strips.

HECK DOOR

The heck door was divided horizontally, so as to allow the lower part to remain closed, yet admit fresh air and light. This is still occasionally seen as a back door for cottages.

PANELLED DOOR

Panelled doors were invented during the Tudor period for opulent houses, and later continued in more general use, becoming ever more elaborate and detailed. Originally they had only two panels that were raised in profile (fielded), and carved and moulded, but as time went on the number of panels increased to six.

TRANSITIONAL DOOR

The transitional door was a cross between a batten door and a panelled door, being battened behind and panelled on the front.

INTERNAL DOORS

Internal doors were largely non-existent in the Tudor period, but, if present, would have been battened, and possibly carved in a linenfold pattern.

DOOR FURNITURE

Hinges
Harr-hinges consisted of dowels fashioned from projecting parts at one side of the top and bottom of the door, that fitted corresponding holes in the lintel and sill.

The strap and pin hinge (strap-hinge) became popular after the Tudor period. A length of iron (strap) was attached to the door, which hung on a pin fixed to the frame.

The iron 'H' hinge was made up of two parts, each one corresponding to the verticals in the H. One was fixed to the door, the other to the frame, and they were connected by means of a rotatable joint, corresponding to the bar in the H. The plates (legs) were decorative, sometimes fashioned into 'S' shapes.

Fastenings

Doors were initially fastened by a horizontal bar (also known as a stang, slot or spar) on the inside, with no handle on the outside. On the earliest types, the bar was fastened to the door frame on a pin, allowing it to rotate, and thus be raised and lowered. The end of the bar slotted into an L-shaped wooden housing on the opposite door frame. Later, the bar was shortened and fixed to the door only, so that it was only necessary to raise it enough to clear the receiver before the door could open. The wooden latch, or sneck, worked on the same principle, but a string attached to the bar also allowed it to be raised from the outside; this was later superseded by the iron latch, operated from the outside by a large iron ring.

The first bolts operated along similar lines, except that the bar was not raised and lowered, but moved sideways, sliding into a receiver in the door frame.

Door Surrounds

Architraving was normally found on external rather than internal doors.

4

Tools and Materials

GENERAL MATERIALS

The two sheet materials most commonly used when constructing dolls' houses are medium-density fibreboard (MDF) and plywood – usually one or a combination of both is chosen for the main panels, interior walls and floors. Chipboard is a somewhat softer, cruder material, unsuited to accurate measurement and fixings, whilst blockboard is made up of two sheets of veneer sandwiching assorted pieces of solid timber. Either chipboard or blockboard might be considered for a base, but not for structural components.

Timber battening and mouldings of various sizes are ideal for exterior timber framing, or interior ceiling-beams and other embellishments. In addition there are types of malleable clay that dry hard and can be moulded to form bricks, tiles or other decoration; fillers are used to bridge gaps and cover screw-head depressions. Metals can be useful for windows and fireplace construction. Fixing devices may also be considered as hardware – screws, pins and hinges, plus adhesives of various kinds.

Paints are often best applied before construction is completed, so as to minimise 'bleeding' of one colour over another when the two are juxtaposed.

When an adhesive or tool is also known by another name, this second term is given in brackets.

SUPPLIERS

Most of the materials you are likely to need are sold in DIY or hardware stores. A few of the more specialist items are only available from model shops (the type that sell equipment for model railway and air-craft constructors), art/graphics material suppliers, or dolls' house retailers. Dolls' house shops often sell a range of specialist items and will usually give helpful guidance. Where an item is only normally available from specialist outlets it is marked with an (S). The photographs in this chapter of dolls' house shop items by courtesy of Doll's House Junction, Kent

SHEET MATERIALS

MDF

MDF is now ubiquitous, used to make furniture, skirting boards, cupboards, and many other items. It is brown in colour, and made from softwood forest thinnings, bonded with an adhesive into sheet form. The thinner types were originally known as 'hardboard', and used only for non-structural decorative panelling, but 9mm (⅜in) thickness and above is tough enough for many general miniaturist building purposes.

Benefits
- Perfect, even surface-finish – no splits or knots.

- Less prone to warp than plywood.
- Because it is of an equal density through-out, it is easy to cut and drill, and can be carved and routed (cutting a groove with a machine), useful when making window shutters or panelled doors. The edge is smooth, unlike the craggy, pitted cross-sectional view of cheaper-grade plywood.
- Bonds easily to itself and other timbers with PVA wood glue.

Drawbacks

- Lacks intrinsic strength; has a tendency to crumble under pressure.
- Will not grip nails – the special 'chip-board thread' screws to be used need a correctly-sized pilot hole to avoid the danger of splitting. These screws grip well when inserted in the flat panel, but are less successful when inserted in edge grain, although they are ade-quate when used in conjunction with glue.
- Heavier than plywood.

Thicknesses

Standard thicknesses: 3mm (⅛in), 6mm (¼in), 9mm (⅜in), 12mm (½in). Thicker sheets are unlikely to be of relevance to dolls' house construction. Available in sheets sized 2440 × 1220mm (8 × 4ft), 1830 × 610mm (6 × 2ft) and 610 × 610mm (2 × 2ft).

Safety

MDF dust is extremely fine and could cause irritation. For this reason it is rec-ommended that when cutting, routing or power-sanding the material, a face mask with a filter designed for wood dust should be worn, and the working area should be ventilated.

PLYWOOD

Plywood is manufactured from several thin sheets of timber bonded together, its cross-section showing dark and light sections. It varies considerably in quality of surface-finish, colour and price. Birch is the best quality, and has a light-coloured, close-grained surface-finish and a tough, firmly-compacted cross-sectional edge. Cheaper types of plywood are usually darker in colour (often reddish), more crumbly in cross-section, with a less regular surface-finish.

Benefits

- Strong and robust – will grip screws and pins fairly well, even in edge grain.
- The timber grain surface makes it ideal for replicating timber surfaces, for example floorboards or wall panels.
- Readily accepts wood stain and wood varnishes.
- Bonds easily to itself and other timbers with PVA wood glue.

Drawbacks

- The timber grain is readily discernible, even after painting. To achieve a flawless finish, grain must be filled with 'fine filler' (*see* page 47) before painting.
- Edges can be uneven and pockmarked with tiny holes which also need to be filled if they are to be displayed.
- Warping is a definite problem, especially over large areas or if the sheet has been stored incorrectly.
- Surface-finish can, rarely, be flawed by woodworm exit holes and knots. Check for these before buying.

Thicknesses

Standard thicknesses: 3mm (⅛in), 6mm (¼in), 9mm (⅜in), 12mm (½in). Thicker

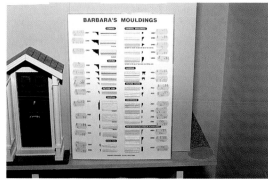

Fig. 48   Specific items for making dolls' houses are available from specialist dolls' house shops.

sheets are unlikely to be required. Available in sheets sized 2440 × 1220mm (8 × 4ft), 1830 × 610mm (6 × 2ft) and 610 × 610mm (2 × 2ft).

Special range of thicknesses (S): 0.8mm (1/32in) and 1.5mm (1/16in), useful for roof tiles or wall panels. Available in sheets sized 305 × 305mm (12 × 12in) or larger.

CARDBOARD

Cardboard can be useful for making roof tiles or floor tiles. Art materials suppliers stock a wide range of thicknesses/grades.

ACETATE SHEETS(S)

Acetate is a form of clear plastic, ideal for windows, as it is safer and easier to cut

than glass. The small sheets (300 × 210mm/11¾in × 8¼in) available from model shops are thinner and easier to cut than the thick acetate sheets stocked by DIY stores and used for secondary double glazing.

TIMBER

TIMBER MOULDINGS

Timber mouldings are available in a variety of cross-sectional profiles; the best are usually made from a hardwood called ramin.

Dowel is cylindrical, sized according to its diameter, whilst quadrant has the cross-sectional profile of a quarter-circle. There is a wide range of picture-frame mouldings, some with cross-sectional profiles that form a right-angled triangle with the third side partly flat and partly curved.

The most frequently used mouldings for exterior decoration have a square- or rectangular-section profile. For interiors, a plate rack rail above wainscoting could easily be simulated using a suitable type of picture-frame moulding. All mouldings can be stuck on to MDF or plywood surfaces, and do not need to be screwed or pinned.

BALSA WOOD(S)

Balsa wood is soft, light spongy timber that can be cut with a craft knife. It can be carved and sanded very easily, but has no structural strength.

METALS

PIANO WIRE(S)

The hardened surface of this thin steel rod means that it can only be cut by 'snapping' it with the slot on the side of some types of pliers, or by grinding it with a metal cutting wheel.

STEEL WIRE

This wire is bendable, and is usually galvanised.

METAL GARDEN MESH

Galvanised panels of steel wire in a mesh can be useful for forming the cames for leaded light windows, creating either diagonal or square cells.

BRASS(ES)

Lengths of hollow tubing, either of square, L-shaped, channel, or round cross-section, from 1.5mm (¹⁄₁₆in) diameter upwards. The soft metal can easily be cut using a junior hacksaw, or a precision razor saw. It can be soldered using an ordinary soldering iron (*see* Chapter 8).

Brass wire is bendable, and can be soldered to the sections above, especially suitable for making imitation caming and window sills. Fire-dogs and andirons can also be made up in this way. Flat strips of the metal are available, as are sheets sized 254mm × 100mm (10in × 4) and solid brass rods.

HARDENING MATERIALS

FILLING COMPOUNDS

Proprietary brands of filler are sold in DIY stores for filling gaps in plaster or wood. Normally ready-mixed in plastic tubs, the compounds are either white or grey in colour, made with an evaporating water-based solvent. They can be smoothed with a knife whilst wet to produce an even surface-finish, or left proud of the surface and smoothed flush afterwards.

Fine surface-filler is made with fine particles of inert filler, and is used for filling the grain surface of timber, or filling very small gaps neatly and precisely. It is easy to sand when dry, and best left proud of the surface. It is also quick drying. Often an unpainted surface can look perfectly smooth, and it is only when painted that the grain texture or unevenly-filled depressions become apparent in a certain light. If in doubt about the smoothness of a surface, the application of fine surface-filler that is well-sanded afterwards is the only way to ensure a good finish.

WOOD FILLERS

Wood fillers are air-drying pastes, available in a range of timber colours. They are suitable for invisibly filling holes in ply or moulding that is to be later sealed with clear varnish.

MODELLING CLAY

There are two types of modelling clay. The first is air-hardening, and is intended for larger projects such as modelling bricks on fireplaces, flagstone floors, or 'carved' stone fire surrounds. The second type needs to be dried in an oven, and would only be suitable for small parts of a dolls' house project.

PLASTER

Plaster of Paris can be bought from a chemist, and can be used for casting plaster designs from moulds, for example pargeting designs on a house exterior. These moulds can be made from special re-meltable rubber, or silicone rubber, which is available from specialist model shops or from sculpture materials suppliers. Alternatively, plaster casts can be made from plaster moulds, provided a suitable release agent is used, for example washing-up liquid, and there are no undercuts (complicated shapes preventing release) on the original item being moulded.

GLASS-REINFORCED PLASTIC (GRP)

Developed for the motor industry, this is a type of yellow-coloured plastic (polyester resin) that remains as a treacly liquid until the addition of a catalyst, which triggers a chemical reaction resulting in the free-flowing material becoming solid. It will bond to metal, timber, and other glass-fibre compounds.

The three main uses of GRP are as follows:

(1) To impregnate white fibrous mats made up of strands of glass. A solvent in the polyester allows the glass fibres to separate from their binding medium so that they can float freely in the liquid. When the polyester becomes hard (cured), the glass is locked into a continuous solid sheet. One disadvantage is that the cured result can not easily be shaped or carved. It has limited use for miniaturists, but could be used for fabricated large panels. The freshly-made material possesses no rigidity whatsoever, so panels are usually cast against moulds, or, if unsupported, perforated zinc sheets can be used to form a temporary rigid surface over which to lay the material.

(2) A specially-produced clear-coloured type of polyester resin can be poured either into a casing, or allowed to run on a horizontal surface, and will dry with the appearance of solid glass. Miniaturists sometimes use this to represent water in a moat or stream. It can be used to encapsulate items such as pieces of coal in a fireplace. Ordinary polyester resin cannot be used in this way – if poured into a mould or allowed to cure within a confined area, it will overheat dangerously and dry to a burnt dark orange colour.

(3) Manufacturers add an inert powder to the resin, producing a (usually grey-coloured) paste. This can be used to fill holes and bridge gaps, mainly in metal – ordinary plaster-type filler is better for wood-based materials.

Unlike ordinary filler, this cannot be shaped while wet – smoothing its surface will only produce a depression, and is liable to raise spikes. As it dries it is apt to change shape, so a second coat is often required. Because it cures by chemical reaction from within, any depth can be used and the whole mass will dry at the same time. Plaster-type fillers are usually water-based, relying on the evaporation of water to dry, therefore there is usually a maximum thickness to which these can be applied. The catalyst is also a paste, making the compound easy to mix together. It can be filed and sanded afterwards, but be prepared to add a second coat in case the sanding reveals holes.

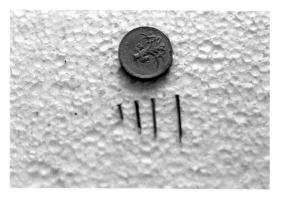

Fig. 49   Tiny nails.

FIXING DEVICES

PANEL PINS

A halfway stage between a pin and a nail, these slim fixings are designed to cause minimum damage to fine-grained timber. Nevertheless, if they are not carefully inserted they can split the side grain of plywood, and do not always provide a specially good grip. Their small heads are easily punched below the timber's top surface, leaving a minimal, easily-filled depression. They cannot be used successfully with MDF.

SCREWS

Use the 'chipboard' type of screw in either MDF or ply; some conventional screws have a proportion of their upper shank unthreaded, and are not intended for fixing relatively thin panels to one another. Most now have Pozidrive or Phillips heads

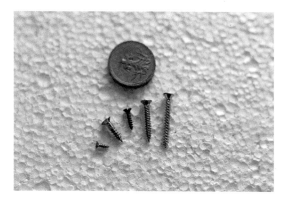

Fig. 50   Tiny screws.

(that is they have a cross-shaped slot), and should be countersunk – domed-head screws are meant to sit above metal surfaces. UK diameter sizes are measured by numbers, ranging from No.1 (almost microscopic) to No.14 (large), and in length from 6mm (¼in) upwards. For assembling exterior panels, floor and wall dividers, using 9mm (⅜in) MDF or plywood, a reasonable size of screw would be a one-inch No.4. Screws are usually rust-proofed, termed 'bright finish'. Hinges are likely to need brass screws, which are

Fig. 51   Hinges.

available in the smallest sizes of all, and are very soft, with 'slots' in the heads because a cross-head would be impractical on such a tiny area.

HINGES

These are usually brass. The largest size likely to be used is 50mm (2in), for house front opening sections. The conventional type has two plates joined by a centrally-raised spine containing a pin. Another type has a smaller square panel that hinges from inside a larger panel. Piano hinges are one long continuous strip of hinge, in either brass-finish thin steel or plastic. The smallest conventional hinges are made of brass-finish steel, and are sold with tiny pins for fixing. The size of the pins and the impracticability of driving them home means that it is often necessary to either stick them in place or drill the hole larger and use tiny brass screws instead.

ADHESIVES

Adhesives are either 'wetstick' – both surfaces are coated with glue and then brought together while the glue is wet, or 'drystick' – a layer of the adhesive is allowed to dry on both surfaces before they are brought together.

PVA WOOD ADHESIVE ('WHITE GLUE') – WETSTICK

The most useful adhesive of all, being incredibly strong, clean and flexible. Be sure to use the type formulated specially for wood, since this is more viscous than the type of PVA adhesive designed for cardboard and paper. The liquid must penetrate both porous timber surfaces, so it is essential that no paint or varnish layer is present on either.

A good bonding is dependent on strong suction being created between the two porous timber surfaces. If one or both of the pieces to be joined are not heavy, simply apply adhesive to both surfaces and press the two together, making sure you feel a suction bond form between them. If the weight of one of the pieces, or other factors such as fractional warping, means that there are even minor forces drawing the surfaces apart so that no good suction bond can form, they must be firmly clamped in place until the glue has dried. There are instances where clamping is impractical and no suction bond can be formed, or else painted timber cannot be stripped; in these cases another kind of adhesive should be used.

Benefits
- Clean, neat, non-toxic, non-flammable, pleasant neutral odour.
- Easy to use.
- Water-based, therefore spills can be removed with a damp cloth.
- Inexpensive.

Drawbacks
- Only suitable for porous materials, for example timber, card or paper,

although some manufacturers claim it can be used for some plastics.

- Joints sometimes have to be clamped, and this is not always practical.
- Surfaces must be cleaned back to bare timber.

Typical applications
- Assembling the main shell of a house.
- Sticking the external timbers in position (no need for clamping).
- Fixing unpainted mouldings in place.

CONTACT ADHESIVE: SOLVENT-BORNE NEOPRENE – DRYSTICK

A fawn-coloured gel based on polychloroprene rubber, that will stick porous and non-porous, painted and non-painted surfaces of most types. Both cleaned surfaces are coated with adhesive which is allowed to dry, after which they are brought together. A powerful 'grab' locks the two instantly in place. If pulled apart at this stage, a web of fine glutinous strands will be apparent, still bonding the two materials. It is available as a liquid or thick gel.

Benefits
- A very strong, instantly gripping bond – no need to clamp.
- Suitable for porous and non-porous surfaces.
- Will stick painted surfaces – no need to sand off surface-finishes.

Drawbacks
- Tends to spread to hands and work surfaces – spills are hard to remove without special solvent cleaner (acetone or nail-varnish remover).
- Strong chemical odour.
- Flammable (do not smoke while using the adhesive).

- The adhesive does not penetrate the materials' surfaces, and is therefore not as permanent or strong as an adhesive such as PVA, that penetrates into wood grain. The bond is, however, adequate for most purposes.
- When used on painted surfaces, the subsequent bond can obviously only ever be as good as the adhesion of the paint itself.

Typical application
- Fixing a painted staircase to an interior wall – strength is required and screws are impractical.

CLEAR ADHESIVE: SOLVENT-BORNE, BASED ON NITRILE RUBBER – DRYSTICK, OCCASIONALLY WETSTICK

Similar to neoprene, but colourless, with a sweeter, less pungent odour and cleaner to use. Non-porous surfaces require it to be used as a drystick, but on porous surfaces it can sometimes be used as a wetstick, applied to one surface only.

Benefits
- Any glue that oozes out from the joint dries to a colourless, non-staining, non-lumpy film that is easily overpainted.
- It is quick drying – on porous surfaces only one surface needs to be coated and the joint can be united immediately (wetstick).
- Although it sticks tenaciously to skin, spills can often be rubbed from materials relatively easily.

Drawbacks
- Not as strong a bond as neoprene, therefore unsuitable where a high-strength bond is required.

- Expensive if used over large areas – more suitable for small-scale fixings.
- Flammable.

Typical application
- Bonding painted ceiling-beams to a painted ceiling.

EPOXY RESIN – WETSTICK

A thick viscous paste comprising two tubed components that are mixed in equal quantities and applied to both surfaces. The resin cures by chemical reaction, rather than by evaporation of solvent or water, and there are two types available: fast setting (10–30 minutes) and slow setting (several hours).

Benefits
- Bonds most materials, porous or non-porous.
- One of the most powerful adhesives known.
- Fills minor cavities.
- Will permanently bond items that nothing else will stick satisfactorily, for example metal to metal, or metal to wood.

Drawbacks
- The joint must be supported (not clamped) until the adhesive has set.
- There is no immediate suction bond (grab), as with contact or clear adhesives.
- It is expensive and therefore unsuitable for large-scale applications.
- Even the 'quick curing' type is slow to dry in comparison with other glues.
- It is hard to remove from hands.

Typical application
- Gluing a metal hinge to the edge of a wooden door.

CYANOACRYLATE ('SUPER GLUE') – WETSTICK

Drying by reaction with atmospheric moisture, a single drop of this colourless watery liquid plus a momentary hand pressure will bond most materials permanently in seconds. Principally designed for non-porous materials (metals, plastics), it is also fine for close-grained timber. Different formulations are available for different materials, for example glass, metals and plastics. It is sold either as a liquid or gel – the treacly non-drip gel has a slightly slower drying time, allowing for any necessary repositioning.

Benefits
- An excellent bond in seconds.
- Ideally suited to small-scale craftwork.
- Clean and neat.
- Sticks many types of plastic.

Drawbacks
- Cleanliness is absolutely vital – any oil or moisture, even sweat from your fingers, will stop the bond. Areas to be bonded must be thoroughly cleaned back to bare surfaces immediately prior to sticking.
- It is no good for very porous materials, but works for some types of timber.
- It will only work on very close-fitting joints, and has no gap-filling properties whatsoever.
- It is expensive, and therefore only viable for small, limited applications.

Typical application
- Making delicate timber furniture or window frames which are too small to permit the use of screws or clamping.

Safety

This type of adhesive can stick skin together, and has even been used successfully as impromptu 'handcuffs'. It normally wears off naturally, but in rare circumstances emergency treatment may be needed for removal from skin.

PAINTS AND OTHER SURFACE TREATMENTS

PRIMER – OIL-BASED

A primer is required on bare wood or metal surfaces prior to painting. Timber primers are usually white, metal primers are often grey.

EMULSION

A water-based paint that dries to a matt or silk (between matt and gloss) finish.

GLOSS

An oil-based paint that requires an oil-based undercoat.

WOOD STAIN

A spirit-based chemical that penetrates the surface of wood grain to darken it. A surface can never be made lighter, but can always be made darker.

VARNISH

Polyurethane seal is a clear yellowy liquid that 'seals in' a stain and gives it a shiny gloss surface; it can also seal unstained timber. Any light-coloured timber will normally darken fractionally when varnished, and the beauty of the grain is usually revealed.

Fig. 52   A wide range of wallpapers, floor and roof decorative papers available from specialist dolls' house shops.

Fig. 53   House wiring kit and other lighting accessories available from specialist dolls' house shops.

TEXTURED COATING MATERIAL

A plaster-based finish intended for interior DIY purposes. Useful for replicating a stipplecast finish on house exteriors.

WALLPAPER

A very wide range of wallpaper, floor and roof-tile papers is available from specialist dolls' house shops.

Fig. 54   Range of lamps available from specialist dolls' house shops.

Fig. 55   Decorative lamps with porcelain shades and other miniature items available from specialist dolls' house shops.

LIGHTING

Electric lighting kits, fittings and lamps are available from specialist dolls' house shops in a huge variety of styles. Running from a transformer plugged into the mains, the special cable is designed for fitting unobtrusively along or behind a wall.

TOOLS

The majority of tools needed are standard DIY hand tools. The only power tools that are necessary are a jigsaw and an electric drill. Where a particular tool is likely to be rarely used, and may not be worth obtaining unless required for a particular project, it is marked 'NV' (not vital).

SAWS

- A hand saw for cutting large timber battens.
- A fine-toothed tenon saw for cutting small mouldings.
- A large hacksaw with a 21-teeth-per-inch hardened steel blade for cutting steel screws or metal.
- Junior hacksaw for either small-scale metal-cutting or delicate woodwork.
- A razor saw (NV) for small-scale work.
- A jigsaw with fine wood-cutting blades – the large-toothed type sold for general timber work is likely to be too inaccurate and crude for precise cutting.
- A fretsaw (NV). This is a thin-bladed saw in a large, deep-throated rectangular frame, for cutting shapes within a wood or metal panel. A carefully-controlled jigsaw can do the same job, but some may prefer the greater degree of accuracy attainable with this hand tool.
- A precision mitre saw (NV) is a saw-and-runner mechanism incorporated within a cutting box, and is much more accurate than a conventional mitre box. It is worth obtaining if you envisage doing much mitring work (often needed for making window frames). Tudor dolls' houses require less accurate mitring work than Georgian-style houses.

Fig. 56   Saws (top to bottom): cross-cut saw, tenon saw, hacksaw, junior hacksaw.

JACK PLANE

A large plane for general large-scale smoothing of un-planed (un-wrought) timber battens, and also ideal for establishing a perfectly straight edge along a sheet of plywood or MDF.

SMOOTHING PLANE

Shorter than the jack plane, the smoothing plane is used for removing high spots, trimming edges and for other small-scale work.

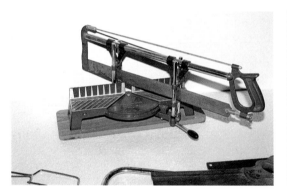

Fig. 57   Precision mitre saw.

Fig. 59   Smoothing plane.

Fig. 58   Jack plane (top), smoothing plane (bottom).

Fig. 60   Top to bottom: Jack plane, smoothing plane, large and small spokeshaves.

55

SPOKESHAVE (NV)

A tool to be used two-handed for carving and slicing away sharp edges. It is used more for artistic work than accurately-measured, precise projects.

CHISELS

Chisels should be kept sharp enough to cut timber by hand pressure alone, or occasionally by knocking the handle with the bony part of the hand. Never use a mallet for this purpose; chisels designed to be used with a mallet are specially strengthened, and are intended for less specialized, more general carpentry work. The most useful sizes of chisel are 6mm (¼in) and 38mm (1½in), however 9mm (⅜in), 12mm (½in), 19mm (¾in) and 25mm (1in) chisels are worth buying if you plan to do much dolls' house construction. Curved-blade chisels can also come in handy, but are only worth buying if the need arises. A gouge is a chisel with a 'V'-shaped blade (NV).

OILSTONE

Used to sharpen plane-irons and chisels.

G-CLAMPS

A minimum of two 150mm (6in) and two 254mm (10in) clamps are needed, for pressing together joints to be bonded with PVA adhesive. Smaller clamps are also useful.

ELECTRIC HAND DRILL

A drill with variable speed is best, but any kind will do. A selection of HSS (high-speed steel) drill bits, plus a countersink bit are also necessary.

Fig. 61   Top: sash clamp, G-clamp, large vice; Left to right: pin-hammer, claw hammer, mallet and mole grips.

VICE

A vice with timber-cushioned jaws is preferable. If you have a steel-jawed vice there are usually bolt holes to allow for screwing blocks of wood against the jaw's surfaces.

MOLE GRIPS (NV)

Mole grips are pliers that effectively lock in place around an item. Principally designed for mechanics and plumbers. they are very useful for holding small items while drilling, soldering or sanding.

SCREWDRIVERS

Large, medium and small ordinary screwdrivers, plus large and small Phillips/Pozidrive-headed types will be needed. An electric screwdriver can save a lot of time when assembling/dismantling a screwed-construction house.

TRY-SQUARE

A medium and a small try-square will be needed to mark lines on panels at right angles to the edge. You will probably use

Fig. 62 Right: Try-squares, large, medium and small; Left: marking gauge (top), bevel gauge (middle), dividers (bottom).

this more than almost any other tool, and the importance of its accuracy cannot be overstressed (panels not cut at right angles mean that the house will be impossible to assemble). Rough handling can affect the set of the blade, so if you are using an old one, ensure it is correctly set, and if out of true, buy another.

BEVEL-SQUARE (SLIDING BEVEL) (NV)

Similar to the try-square, except that the angle of the blade is fully adjustable, allowing the transference of a particular angle to another medium.

MARKING GAUGE

A marking gauge scribes lines a measured distance from, and parallel to, the edge of timber and saves hours of measurement.

RULES

- Retractable tape rule.
- Long (1m/39in) flat steel rule or woodworker's foldable wooden rule.
- Ordinary (300mm/12in) flat steel rule.
- Small (150mm/6in) steel rule.

BRADAWL

A steel-pointed shaft held in a wooden handle with a variety of uses, including marking, grooving floorboards and identifying screw destinations. Different kinds of points are available – find the sharpest you can.

PENCILS

A 2H pencil for accurate measurement marking and an HB for freehand identification and panel marking are needed.

OTHER HAND TOOLS

- Hammer.
- Very small hammer (for panel pins).
- Metal file.
- Pliers and pincers.
- Sharp craft knife with replaceable blades, or blades that can be sharpened.
- Sandpaper (coarse, medium and fine).
- Paint brushes.
- A mallet – useful for tapping panels into position.

HELPFUL (NV) TOOLS

- Electric orbital sander – this saves time when sanding flat panels.
- Sash clamps – long (1830mm/6ft) heavy steel strips with fully adjustable end-pieces attached, designed to act like huge 'jaws'. or giant G-clamps, that can compress a very wide panel. They are used when making items of furniture for example.
- Tweezers – often fingers are too large to manipulate tiny components or pieces of wood/metal.
- Razor saw —a very small, fine-bladed saw (42-teeth-per-inch) for accurately cutting either timber or metal to an exceptionally high degree of accuracy,

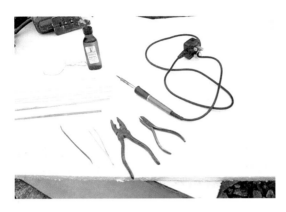

Fig. 63   Soldering equipment and materials: Brass extrusions (left); Bottom left to right: file, tweezers, pliers, tin snips; Soldering iron (right); flux and solder (top left).

when making dolls' house furniture for example.

- Soldering iron – for soldering together brass or copper component parts, such as when making a fireplace grate, fire-dogs or a kitchen range.

SPECIALIST TOOLS FOR ADVANCED OR INTRICATE PROJECTS (NV)

Lathe
A lathe revolves pieces of timber at high speed so that a chisel held against the spinning timber will trim it evenly around its circumference. Lathe attachments are available that can be powered by an ordinary electric drill.

Router
A motorised tool similar to a drill, but with a flat bed behind the cutting spindle. Passing a length of timber over, or to one side of, the spindle cuts away a precisely-shaped channel. Can be used for making slots along the faces of panels. For example when fixing a floor between two side walls, a channel can be cut into the side panels to accept the edges of the floor.

Electric Drill Stand
A table (bed) with an upright pillar on which a drill can be fixed. A handle allows the drill to be raised or lowered, so that holes can be accurately drilled in items placed on the bed.

Electric Fretsaw
Comprises a metal cutting table with a central hole, through which an exceptionally thin blade goes up and down. The work is placed flat on the table and pushed against the blade, allowing intricate curves and shapes to be cut from wood or metal. Alternatively, the blade can be inserted through a pre-drilled hole so that variously shaped holes can be cut within a panel. It is also useful for slicing timber into strips.

MINI POWER TOOLS (NV)

A range of miniature tools powered by a drill that is only 150mm (6in) long. The drill can reach parts inaccessible to an ordinary electric drill. A full range of drill bits, sanders and polishers is available.

- Drill stand, on which a 'shaper table' can rest, allowing the use of cutting tools in the drill for slicing out shapes and rebates.
- Drum and orbital sanders.
- Mini lathe – used to make miniature turned chair legs for example (powered by drill).
- Horizontal drill holder (for 'hands-free' sanding and polishing).
- Router (powered by drill).

5

Preparing Plans

SCALE

A popular and practical scale for building a dolls' house is 1:12, and this corresponds to most of the available furniture. However, growing in popularity with adult miniaturist collectors is the smaller 1:24 size, and anyone interested in building to this scale will find *Small-Scale Modelling* by Caroline Osborne (The Crowood Press), of value. A scale of 1:6, where a three-storey house would be approximately five feet high, will mean a large and heavy dolls' house, but is perfect for anyone making a scale replica of an actual house, or who enjoys modelling on a grand scale. A scale of 1:16 tends to be followed for mass-produced dolls' houses.

IMPERIAL OR METRIC

Since measurements can be intricate and complicated, some people find it more logical and simpler to use metric, since fractions of an inch can be confusing, and the smallest metric unit, the millimetre, is probably also the smallest practical size that can be easily measured. Cutting timber to within a millimetre of accuracy is certainly precise enough for most houses.

Those who are more comfortable with imperial measurements will already be familiar with eighths and sixteenths of an inch, however, and would rather continue to think in these dimensions. It is always better to decide whether to use metric or imperial at the beginning of a project, then stick to the same choice throughout, so as to avoid possible confusion.

PLANNING

Begin with photographs of an actual house, or postcards, or drawings from a book. Alternatively, anyone adept at sketching will be able to make an accurate drawing of a building. It is a fine idea to dream up the general concept of your house, but a scale drawing, or better still a photograph, shows the relationship between different areas. Small photos, drawings or postcards should be magnified by photocopying to a size large enough to take measurements from. If nothing is readily available, your library is bound to have books on architecture, or even scenery pertaining to towns, which may have pictures of houses. Particular 'Tudor' areas seem to be Kent and parts of Suffolk and Essex, but practically all areas in the UK are likely to feature some Tudor buildings.

The front façade is the most important view. It is vital to ensure that all proportional relationships are correct, particularly that between the height of the roof and that of the upper and lower storeys. A problem with perspective occurs, but this is not likely to matter much, as long as corresponding parts are made the same width in your plan, for example the width of the right and left wings of a Wealden house.

Next, draw out a rough plan (an elevation) of the front façade. Measure the size and width of each component part, as well as window and door openings, and mark everything on the paper. Again, metric measurements are easiest, because the fractions inherent to imperial measurement make the subsequent calculations difficult. There is no need to stick to metric afterwards if you prefer imperial – it is simply a question of converting the metric measurements to imperial at the building drawing stage.

ASSESSING RELATIVE SIZES WHILST PRESERVING PROPORTIONS

Here is a way to create a drawing from a photograph or picture of an actual house. First, choose a part of the building whose actual size is known to you, for example a window or the front door. If you do not know the actual size of either of these, choose a door – ideally the front entrance door – and measure this on the photograph or drawing. Making allowances for the shorter height of Tudor people, assume that the actual door height was 1700mm, whilst on the photograph or drawing this height is 23mm. This latter measurement would therefore have to be multiplied by a specific number to give the full size of the door, in this case: 1700 divided by 23 = 74. If your scale is 1:12, the door height for the dolls' house should be 1700 divided by 12 = 142mm.

Therefore to simplify calculations it makes sense to divide the multiplying figure of 74 by 12, and to multiply this new figure, 6.17, by the measurement on the diagram; 6.17 multiplied by 23mm = 142mm, the size of the dolls' house door. Every measurement on the diagram is then

multiplied by the 'scaling up figure', in this case 6.17, and will thus be in proportion, just as it is in your original photograph or drawing.

For other scales, just divide the multiplying figure accordingly. For example, for a 1:6 scale it would be 12.33 (74 ÷ 6), and for 1:24 it would be 3.08 (74 ÷ 24).

A problem with drawings and photographs is likely to be that there is either a corner view, showing only part of the side, or else the side view is foreshortened because of perspective. In this case, it is a question of judgement and guesswork, but knowing the likely shape of the rooms will help to assess this with a good enough degree of accuracy.

Having noted the calculated dolls' house dimensions on the rough drawing, draw the whole thing to scale to check that everything looks in proportion, and is as you had envisaged. Draw a front elevation, both side elevations and a back elevation. Remember that although it is a good idea to try to retain accurate architectural proportions, you may want to alter and adapt various windows, room sizes or roof slopes. The actual height of the roof is apt to be almost as high as the ground floor and the first floor combined, and you may want to have a shallower roof for practical reasons.

A good dolls' house with play value might be very different from a precision-made architectural model, and between these two extremes lie a variety of options. If you have to choose between faithful architectural reproduction and practicality, always go for practicality; it can often be the case that a particular dimension, for example the height of a room, can be acceptable in reality but look totally awkward and impractical in small scale. Bear in mind the size and height of any furniture that you may have, or wish to make or buy later on. Imagining furniture within the rooms can be an excellent way of assessing correct dimensions.

Once you have made scale drawings, you may then want to make a scale cardboard model, again to check that proportions and room sizes are as you wish. Alternatively, the drawings will probably give you a perfectly good idea of the finished house.

PERSPECTIVE DRAWINGS

Presenting a three-dimensional object in two dimensions can be a helpful way of assisting you to visualise the finished concept and decide such aspects as how and where doors should open, and the positions of chimneys. Anyone who can draw perspectives will know how the practice quickly unlocks ideas, and helps you to zip through a train of thought in order to accept or reject a particular way of constructing something. Regard the practice

of producing ideas as perspectives as a useful, rather than a vital, tool in your design. Some people prefer to make actual scale models instead, whilst others simply find that visualising the building in the mind's eye is adequate.

Two-Point Perspective

The principle is that for any object viewed from a particular angle, some of the lines, if drawn beyond the object, would converge at two points, called vanishing points. In practical terms, this just means that you draw lines 1, 2 and 3 parallel to each other – although according to the diagram the whole point is that they are not exactly parallel, or they would never converge at the vanishing point. In fact, the vanishing point is so far away that you can treat them as parallel. Similarly, lines 4, 5, 6 and 7 are parallel with each other. Draw lines 9, 10, 11, 12 and 13 upright, in line with the side edges of the paper, and draw the roof lines

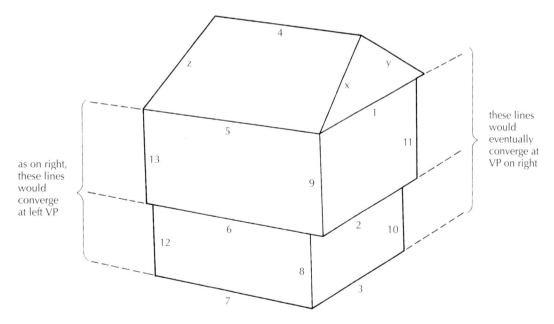

Fig. 64   Two-point perspective.

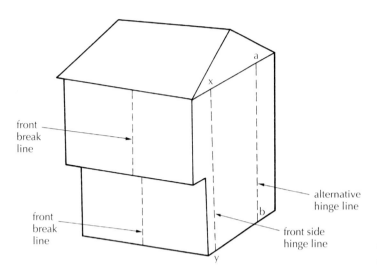

Fig. 65   Ways of hinging a house.

x, y and z according to your own judgement. If you draw a rough and ready freehand sketch first, then use the position of the lines to align everything as above, it can look neat and professional; but, most importantly, will help you to visualise how the house will look in the light of various amendments.

THE MAIN SHELL – GENERAL EXTERNAL CONSIDERATIONS

A number of key decisions have to be made. Assuming you have a good idea of the style of house you want to make – its general shape, and how it appears from the outside – the first thing to consider is how it should open. Front opening is usual, and the first decision is, where should the opening sections hinge from? It has to be somewhere along the side panels.

THE FRONT OPENING

For a front-opening house, the most logical approach is to have a right and a left opening front section, hinged at each side and meeting at some point along the front panel. Subsequently, this meeting point of the right and left opening front section will be called the front break line, and the hinge lines where the panels open from called the side hinge lines.

To illustrate the ramifications of various decisions, imagine you want to have the right-hand side hinge line along the line xy. It will be clear that the hinge line must be stepped back from the upper-storey building line, and the opening must include the jettying at the front. This consideration might mean the constructor would rather have the right front section opening at top floor and ground floor levels separately, meaning there are four front openings instead of two.

Supposing you decide to have the hinge line near the back right-hand side (ab). When the front and side walls swing away, the upper floor will be left more or less dangling in mid-air, and it wouldn't actually be a room – the lack of two walls instead of just one could belittle play value, and furniture would be at risk of falling out. This might not matter, and you might feel that the advantages of being able to open up the house so much would out-weigh the disadvantages.

ROOF

Having chosen from the types of roof available (*see* Chapter 2), it is necessary to decide whether it will open on a hinge at the apex, be totally removable or partially removable.

CHIMNEY(S)

Should the house have one or two chimneys? Should one be an integral part of the roof or fit to the side of the house?

BASE

Should this project underneath the opening front sections? If so, by how much? How will its front edge be finished off, so as not to stand out from the base of the doors?

OTHER EXTERIOR DETAILS

- Exterior timbering – the size of the timbers, their pattern, and details of jett-ying.
- Windows – their size and position, the type of glazing bars, and whether acetate is to be used to represent glass.
- Chimney – the type of chimney and style of brickwork.
- Roof – should it incorporate gables with windows? Which style of roofing material should be used?

THE INTERIOR

The following decisions should be made initially:

- How many floors?
- What height should the floors be, bearing in mind window positions?
- How many rooms should each floor be divided into, and where should these be positioned?
- Where will the stairs be positioned to afford maximum play value and logical approach to all the rooms?
- Where should door openings be placed?

CONSTRUCTION

Sometimes it can be a good idea to make the outer shell as a complete unit, and the inner floors and walls as an interlocking construction that can be slotted into the shell. Another strategy is to build the walls and floors into the empty shell as it is constructed. Each design will vary, and the merits of either method should be evaluated.

Every detail of construction is important when working out the actual size of pieces. For example, if the side panels of the main shell are fixed against the back panel, the overall length of the back panel will be the length of the house, minus twice the thickness of the side panels. On the other hand, if the side panels back up against the back panel of the house, its overall length will be the same as that of the house, and each side wall will be narrower by the back wall's thickness. Wherever you plan to have walls within the house, decide on a centre line, then mark the wall's actual position on the floor(s) by subtracting half the wall's thickness either side of this central line, therefore indicating the actual thickness of the wall itself.

PLANNING, FURNISHING AND DECORATING

Wall finishes have to be planned before final house construction, because it is usually far more practical to decorate walls or carve floorboards on the separate panels. A good plan can be to assemble the house initially using screws alone, then dismantle it in order to decorate the walls and floors, and finally reassemble it permanently, using adhesive.

The next key choices to be made regarding the interior include the following:

- Stairs – what type? Will a banister rail be needed?
- Doors – what type?
- Floors – what material should be used

– floorboards, flagstones? Left plain or painted?
- Windows – should the interior framework have a curtain pole, or be left plain?
- Walls – should there be wainscoting – with a plain ledge? Should they simply be painted with emulsion?
- Ceilings – should these have ceiling-beams or just be painted?
- Fireplace(s) – exact position(s) and size(s) should be decided, as these require pre-cut holes in walls and chimney positions.

WORKED EXAMPLE

Below is a straightforward design of a house, showing each stage and how it was reached.

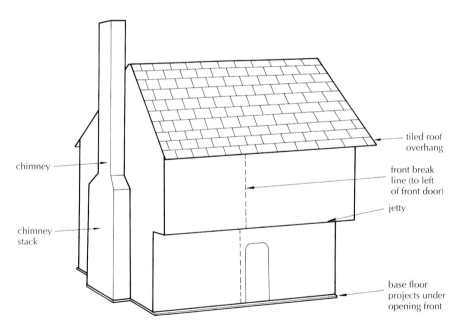

Fig. 66   Outline of proposed house design.

DESCRIPTION

This is a front-jettied Tudor house, with a removable roof, and right and left front-opening sections. The chimney abuts the left-hand wall and the roof incorporates two gables with windows.

The rough working drawing is a decision-making tool that is speedy to produce and totally flexible. You may prefer to make a cardboard model, or even just picture it in your mind and make notes. Any method will do, as long as you're able to reach the requisite decisions in order to go on to the next stage.

CRITICAL DESIGN ASPECTS

- The front right and left sections will be hinged behind the upper-storey projection but closer to the lower-storey wall. This means that each piece will be a 'box' containing the front inch or so of upper-storey floor, and the window reveals (the thickness of wall comprising the sides of the window) will be as deep as this projection.
- The roof will overhang slightly, which means there must be a band of timber above the opening front sections to allow the front sections to open with the roof in position.
- The front part of the roof, plus a piece of overhang over the back will be removable, resting on the ridge bar between the apex of the triangular-topped side walls.
- The front break line is to be to the left of the front door entrance, and a method must be devised to allow for an overlap of right over left section, so as to avoid any gap where the two meet.

INTERIOR DECISIONS

- The house has two rooms on the ground floor, the larger of which contains the stairs (no separate hall).
- The first floor has two rooms, plus a landing for both sets of stairs.
- The upper floor has one very large room, containing the stairwell and another smaller room.
- The width of the stairs pertains to the width of first floor landing.
- The doors are to be towards the front of the house for ease of access.
- The ground floor will be finished with flagstones, both upper floors grooved and stained dark oak, to represent floorboards.
- The inner core will comprise: a first and upper floor, one ground-floor wall, two first-floor walls and one top-floor (triangular) wall.

Extrapolating sizes of the panels from the rough diagram is easy, simply requiring logical thought. Think of the overall size of the rectangular panels and cut these first, afterwards removing further material (as for the side panels) if necessary.

STRUCTURE OF THE BUILDING FRAME

The sides fix to the edges of the back, and this three-sided structure fits around, and is fixed to, the base. It is normally better to enclose the base on three sides in this way, as the alternative – fitting the base to the bottom of the back and walls – is less secure.

Total width = a
Total depth = b
Total height (to apex of roof, excluding thickness of roofing material) = c
Thickness of building material (likely to be 9mm (⅜in)) = m

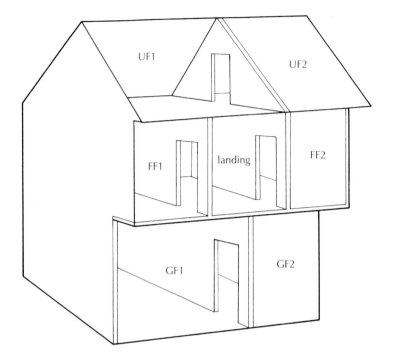

Fig. 67   Interior plan showing rooms.

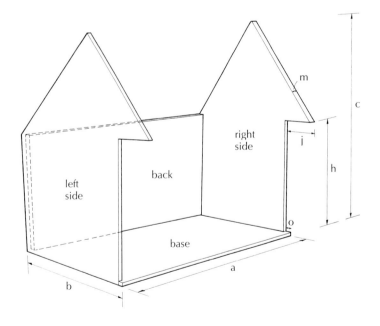

Fig. 68   Main components of house carcase.

66

Height to second-floor top surface = h
Width of outcrop (say 20mm/¾in) = o
Width of jetty overhang = j

Sizes of rectangular pieces to cut, to be trimmed to exact size later:

Side 1 (left) – c × b.
Side 2 (right) – as side 1.
Base a × (b – m + o) (the width is the same as the overall width of the house, and the depth is the overall depth minus thickness of the back (m) plus the width of the outcrop).
Back (a – 2 × m) × h (the width is the width of the house minus the thickness of the left and right side walls (2 × m), and the height is the height to the second-floor top surface (h)).

Trimming the Sides and Base

Sides Measure the length (h) from the base, and mark at both sides. Measure and mark the centre of the top, then join the lines. Draw a line distance j + m measured back from the front edge, terminating at second-floor height; m represents the thickness of the opening front panel.

Base The L-shaped cuts must be (measured from the rear) [b – (j + m)] – m long, and m in width. Disregarding the brackets in the calculation gives the wrong figure.

Walls and Floors

Comprising six panels – first floor, top floor, ground-floor wall, first-floor wall left, first-floor wall right, and top-floor wall.

Height of ground floor (floor-to-ceiling) = x
Height of first floor (floor-to-ceiling) = y
Height of second floor (floor-to-highest point – apex) = z

First floor is therefore: [b – (j + m)] – m wide and a – (2 × m) long.
Top floor is therefore: b – m wide (it includes the jetty overhang) and a – (2 × m) long.

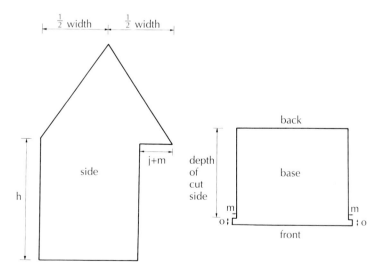

Fig. 69   Trimming sides and base.

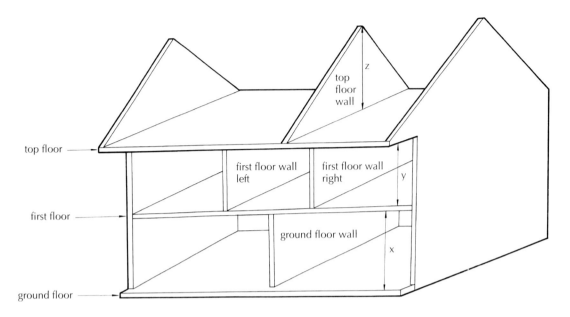

Fig. 70   Establishing sizes of walls and floors.

Ground floor wall is therefore: x high and [b − (j + m)] − m deep.

First floors left and right are therefore both: y high and [b − (j + m)] − m deep.

Top floor wall is therefore: z high and b deep. There is no need to subtract the width of the front panel because it will overlap the back panel of the house, and therefore be of the same dimensions as the top part of the main side panels of the house. The top floor will be cut accordingly, to follow the shape of the sides of the house.

Front Opening Sections and Roof

These are made from a single panel, with the upper jetty section fixed to the front top part of each. The roof is made with a generous overhang at the front, back and sides, the front part of which is removable.

68

— 6 —

Woodwork and Other Craft Techniques

TOOLS

JACK PLANE

This is essentially a heavy metal casing, the underside of which is a perfectly flat horizontal slotted bed. A sharp blade projects through this slot, and its position relative to the bed can be adjusted by a wheel controlling the depth of cut. To set the blade correctly, hold the plane upside down, sight along the bed to see how far the blade protrudes, and rotate the wheel until only a tiny fraction of raised blade can be seen.

Guidelines

Always plane along the whole length of timber in one go, never a part at a time. The guiding hand holds the grip handle, the other hand rests on the rounded knob,

Fig. 71   Using a Jack plane.

exerting a very slight pressure downwards. You may find it helpful to rest your index finger along the side of the tool. As you push the plane along the length of the timber (or MDF or plywood) edge a continuous shaving should appear, curving upwards and out in front of the blade in the slot. If sporadic shavings only are removed, this either means that the timber has high spots which are being removed, or you are not exerting an even pressure. Clear the debris from in front of the blade if any builds up (particularly when working with friable material), and also sharpen the blade regularly. Striking knots can knock the blade backwards, in which case the blade's projection should be readjusted. Always start with the blade hardly showing, then adjust it a fraction at a time. If the blade projects too much it will keep jamming and will not cut properly. Use a smoothing plane in exactly the same way, and the spokeshave two-handed.

CHISEL

Hold the chisel as shown. Hand pressure alone should be enough to slice timber; occasionally it may be necessary to strike the handle with the heel of the other hand.

Guidelines
- Always cut *across* the grain, never along it.
- Use the largest chisel possible.

Fig. 72   Using a chisel – if you guide the blade with your hand, keep all fingers behind the blade.

Fig. 73   Striking chisel with the heel of the hand – do not use a mallet with an ordinary chisel.

- Sharpen it regularly – a blunt chisel can be dangerous and inefficient.
- Always have your other hand *behind* the cutting edge, never in front of it.
- Cut from each side towards the middle rather than straight across – angling the blade upwards can often be helpful. Cutting straight across to the other side usually tears grain away from underneath the cutting line.

Sharpening Plane-Irons and Chisels

These need regular sharpening as they blunt quickly. Only one side of the blade is angled, and this is comprised of two distinct angles: the main slope is at 25 degrees, but the final tip is sharpened at a slightly less steep pitch, to 30 degrees. These angles are judged by eye, and the main 25-degree angle is set using a mechanical grinder, or alternatively a grinding stone driven by an electric drill held in a vice. Since this major 'setting-up angle' only needs to be maintained infrequently, you may find it more convenient to use a blacksmith's shop or a hardware store. The frequent, day-to-day sharpening is of the tip alone, by hand pressure on the oilstone.

Assume the blade is correctly set at 25 degrees, with its edge set square to its length.

(1) Soak the oilstone with thin household lubricating oil. Leave a pool on the surface and keep adding to this throughout the process, its purpose being to float away tiny metal fragments. Never blot up this oil.
(2) Hold the blade against the stone, its angled edge flat to the abrasive face. Blades wider than the stone must be held at an oblique angle.

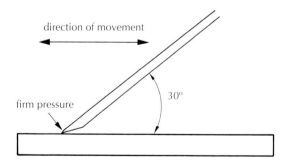

direction of movement

firm pressure

30°

Fig. 74   Sharpening a plane-iron or chisel.

(3) Lift the back of the blade fractionally so as to create a slightly less acute angle.

(4) Whilst pressing down at the front ('firm pressure') with your other hand, push the blade along the stone's length, backwards and forwards several times, maintaining the blade's angle relative to the stone. The slick of oil will turn black, denoting the removal of metal fragments. Use the whole length of the stone and add oil as necessary to keep it permanently wet.

(5) After sharpening, a thin curl of metal projecting behind the blade's edge should be apparent – this is called the swarf. Turn the blade over and place it, flat side down, on the stone. Whilst pressing down from above, slide it from side to side to remove the swarf, taking care not to raise the flat metal from the stone's surface: doing this will destroy the keen edge.

(6) Check the blade's sharpness by gently pushing it against scrap timber – it should glide through the grain of softwood (going with the grain) easily.

HAND-HELD SAWS

When using any kind of non-electric handheld saw, always begin by drawing the blade backwards across the cutting line several times, until it can be pushed forwards with ease. Use the saw's complete length.

Precision Mitre Saw

Hold the work tight against the tool's bed and the rear guard panel. As with other hand-held saws, start by drawing the blade backwards a few times to establish a smooth cutting route.

Jigsaw

Switch the saw on before applying the blade to the work. When the blade starts cutting, press gently in the direction of the line of cut, simultaneously pushing the tool downwards to keep the metal plate hard in contact with the panel, and not allowing it to 'jump' out of the work as a result of the blade's movement. Switch off after removing the tool from the work, not before.

Keep your other hand well away from the blade. Use it to control the panel, but only ever at a substantial distance from the blade. For intricate cutting, hold the work in a vice, or clamp it to the workbench rather than risk cutting near fingers.

Practise curves on scrap material first. Cut to the waste side (*see* page 72) of the marked line, never along it, treating the pencil line as sacrosanct: the oscillating blade will remove a slit about 2mm (3⁄32in) wide, and if part of this is on the line the panel will be cut undersize. It is better to err on the waste side if necessary as excess material can be planed away later. Planing will also remove any dips or hollows.

ELECTRIC DRILL

Switch on before applying the drill to work to allow your hands to adjust to the vibration. A tip for accurate drilling is to make a slight depression with a bradawl at the marked site so that the drill 'finds' it. For a series of holes, go from one to the next without stopping. To drill tiny holes in soft timber, switch on then release the trigger, applying the point as the machine loses speed – this is an aid to precision drilling. When drilling metal, it can be helpful to drill a small hole first and increase this gradually with progressively larger drill bits. When drilling holes to a specific depth, a good idea is to mark this on the drill shank with a piece of masking tape. A countersink bit, used for creating a tapering depression on the surface of a screw's entry hole, so that the screw's head sinks below the timber surface, must be used with care to avoid removing too much material.

JIG

This is a box, normally three-sided with a base, in which structures such as window frames can be assembled individually to ensure that their size will be identical. It is also useful for holding four-sided structures together while waiting for glue to dry. It is usually made from plywood or MDF.

Fig. 75   Using a marking gauge.

TECHNIQUES FOR MEASURING AND MARKING PANELS

The three principle aims are that: (1) the panel dimensions should be accurate; (2) all right angles must be true; (3) edges should be straight, with no discernible dips or high spots.

- Use a 2H pencil with 9mm (⅜in) of lead exposed and sharpened to a flat chisel-type point (use sandpaper), so as to produce an ultra thin line.
- Allow for 9mm (⅜in) of waste between cutting lines, to facilitate cutting on the waste side of each one.
- A retractable steel measure laid flat on the panel is accurate, but a wooden rule must be turned on its edge so that the gradation mark can be matched precisely to the wood's surface; using it flat can lead to parallax errors of judgement.
- If measurement on a wooden or steel ruler starts at zero, it can often be helpful to align its end against the timber's edge, resting both against a fingertip or ball of the thumb to check that the two are in line.
- Use a try-square as a guide where necessary to ensure that measurements taken from a long edge are at right angles to it.
- When cutting plywood take note of the grain direction – it may be of relevance when cutting floors whose top surface is to be carved to represent floorboards.

USING A MARKING GAUGE

This tool is for scratching a line on the surface of timber at a prescribed distance from its edge, for example when marking the line for a row of screw holes. First set the distance between the side of the square block and the scribing point to the required distance. Then, keeping the square block's head tight against the timber's edge, drag it towards you so that the point drags across the timber surface, scratching a line. The accuracy of a gauge set to exactly half the thickness of a panel can be verified by pressing the point into the cross-section from both sides; holes stabbed from both sides should be in the same place.

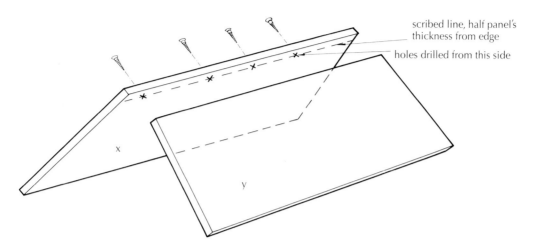

scribed line, half panel's thickness from edge

holes drilled from this side

Fig. 76   Fixing the edges of two panels together with screws.

FIXING THE EDGES OF TWO PANELS TOGETHER WITH SCREWS

MATERIALS

- plywood or MDF, 9mm (⅜in) thickness
- screws – 25mm (1in) No.4 (UK) countersunk chipboard-thread

METHOD

(1) Scribe the inside face of panel X (using the marking gauge) a distance of half the thickness of the panels from the edge.

(2) Drill 2mm (⁵⁄₆₄in) holes at 76mm (3in) centres along this line.

(3) Hold the panels in the correct relative position to each other and mark through one of the drilled holes into the edge of panel Y, using a sharp-pointed bradawl.

(4) Take the panels apart. Clarify this marked site in the edge of panel Y by stabbing it deeper with the bradawl. NB. It is important for these reception hole sites to be exactly in the centre of the panel's thickness, so if the marked depression is off-centre, correct it.

(5) Drill this hole using a 2mm (⁵⁄₆₄in) drill bit to a depth of 15mm (⅝in).

(6) Re-drill the corresponding hole in panel X with a 3mm (⅛in) drill bit.

(7) Screw the panels together.

(8) Mark the positions of the other screw reception holes with the bradawl. Take the panels apart.

(9) After clarifying the reception hole positions, as step 4, drill these newly-marked reception holes in the edge of panel Y, as step 5.

(10) Re-drill the holes in panel X to 3mm (⅛in), then countersink these holes on the outside face.

(11) Screw the panels together. If this is the final assembly (not just tem-

73

porary assembly prior to decoration) apply PVA adhesive to both mating edges before screwing them together.

FIXING THE EDGE OF A PANEL TO THE SURFACE OF ANOTHER

(1) Mark lines to show where the panel's edge will meet the other panel's surface.
(2) On the panel surface, draw a line midway between these outer lines and drill pilot holes, as above.
(3) Mark destination holes as above and proceed as for fixing panels edge-to-edge.

JOINING PANELS USING PANEL PINS

The disadvantage of this method is that the fixing cannot be undone, in order to dismantle a house so that all interior walls and floors can be decorated for example. Other problems include the danger of a pin entering too closely to a panel's edge, causing a bulge, and the fact that they do not grip satisfactorily in the end grain of MDF.

Aside from these factors, this method is perfectly acceptable provided that you always drill a pilot hole in the panel through which the pin enters first. Position the hole so as to coincide with half the panel's thickness, to reduce the possibility of the pin entering off-centre.

A small pin hammer is the best tool to use. Once the pins have been hammered

home, punch their heads below the panel's surface using a nail punch or a large blunted nail.

WEIGHT-BEARING SCREWS AND PLYWOOD/MDF EDGES

The close-fibred grain of softwood or hardwood timber will grip a screw's thread or a nail tightly, but a screw inserted into the fibrous edge of ply or MDF will not grip tightly enough to take any weight, even though screws inserted into the surface of such a panel will grip well. This is of particular relevance if you are mounting hinges for hanging the heavy front opening panel of a dolls' house.

A good way to surmount this problem is by inserting and gluing fillets of ramin or other hardwood into the panel's edge wherever load-bearing screws are to be inserted. Use timber that is slightly thicker than the panel and plane away the surplus later. PVA adhesive is best for plywood, but epoxy resin must be used for MDF.

INSERTING TIMBER FILLETS ALONG PANEL EDGES

Measure and mark the position of the fillet, allowing for it to be slightly proud of the timber's edge afterwards. Cut out the piece as accurately as possible with the jigsaw, making sure that the base line is straight. Alternatively, use a tenon or jigsaw to cut a series of lines within outer perimeter lines, at right angles to the edge, removing the small timber pieces with a sharp chisel afterwards. Glue and insert the fillets, ensuring that they are a tight fit, and, if using PVA adhesive, clamp them in position until the glue has set (sash clamps are ideal for this).

REBATING

A rebate is a step-shaped channel cut into the edge (or surface) of timber. When cutting a rebate for a hinge in the edge of a panel it is usually more practical to cut across the complete thickness of the panel, rather than part of the width. Rebating a hinge means removing timber, equivalent to the thickness of the closed hinge, from the panel's edge as a way of allowing the closed hinge to be recessed into the timber's surface edge. If a hinge rebate is cut too deeply, the door (or opening front section) will not close completely. If it is not cut deeply enough, the door will stand proud.

REBATING A HINGE IN A DOOR'S EDGE

(1) Use a 2H pencil to mark the hinge position precisely on the panel's edge, then, using a small try-square, continue these lines down both panel surfaces.
(2) Using a marking gauge set to the thickness of the closed hinge, mark along the door surfaces to intersect with the lines marked in step 1.
(3) Holding the door in a vice, make a series of saw cuts about 3mm (⅛in) apart, starting with the outer perimeter marked lines (cut *inside* these lines so that the saw's width falls on the waste side). Take care to cut no further down than the marking gauge's scratched line.

(4) Use a small chisel to remove the cut materials, as usual cutting from each side towards the centre.
(5) File the lower surface to ensure a flat, un-pitted surface.

HANGING A DOOR

(1) If using miniature screws, make sure that hinges close completely when the screws are in their respective holes. If the plates are held apart by the screw-heads, countersink the holes carefully using a larger-sized drill bit. The only way to use the tiny nails supplied with the hinges is to pre-drill the holes and stick the nails and back side of the hinge plates using cyanoacrylate adhesive ('Super Glue').
(2) Rebate slots for the hinges on the door's edge, then fix the hinges in place, taking care that the opening side is as planned. The hinge pivot lines must be precisely aligned with the edge of the door, usually meaning that the screws or nails are in the centre of the door's thickness.
(3) Open out the hinges and place the door within its aperture. Mark on the hinge-adjacent wall the exact position of one of the screws for each hinge.
(4) Remove the door from the aperture and continue the marked hinge screw lines inside the door frame.
(5) Delineate the exact position of the screw holes in the door frame and make a small impression in these with a sharp bradawl.
(6) Screw or fix the nails in place and check that the door closes correctly. A slightly tight fit does not matter, and can easily be remedied by removing material along the door's leading edge, using a plane.

(7) If these screw holes are wrong, repeat the procedure using the other holes. Finally fit the remaining two screws.

CARVING MDF

This dense material is well-suited to carving, unlike plywood, whose cross-section is friable and pitted due to the nature of its construction.

Draw the design on the MDF's surface, then use a craft knife with a sharp, pointed blade to make progressively deeper cuts around the areas to be removed. Use a chisel to remove material as required, and finish off with sandpaper.

CHAMFERING FRONT-OPENING PANELS

When front-opening panels meet without overlapping, it can be difficult to cut them

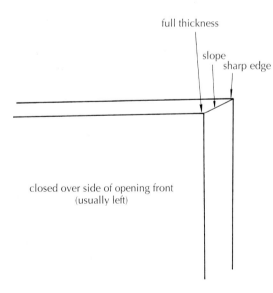

full thickness

slope

sharp edge

closed over side of opening front
(usually left)

Fig. 77   Chamfering front opening panels.

accurately enough to meet without a visible gap. One way round this is to chamfer them (plane off the edges to 45-degree angles), so that the sloping overlap of one fits neatly against the sloping face of the other, and neither stands proud.

For right panel (door) closing over left:

(1) Establish the break line along the house front, then cut the left-hand door longer by the thickness of the panel.
(2) Cut the right-hand door to the length of where the break line occurs.
(3) Hang the doors on both sides. Close the right door over the left and draw a line where it meets the left door. The distance of this line from the door's edge on the left door's *front surface* should be the same as the panel thickness.
(4) Plane away the corner along this edge so that a 45-degree edge is formed, making sure that the marked line is not encroached, and keeping the original bottom-edge line.
(5) In the same way, mark a line the panel's thickness distance away from the *back surface* of the right-hand panel, and chamfer from here.
(6) Ensure that the panels close against each other neatly, planing further if necessary.

MITRING CORNERS

Window frames on Tudor dolls' houses are usually butt-jointed rather than mitred, meaning that the battens simply meet at right angles. But there are likely to be other occasions when mitring is necessary, for example when making framing for wainscoting panels.

Always use a sharp saw.

(1) Mark either the outer or inner point of the line to be mitred, and ensure that the saw goes to the waste side of this.

(2) Whilst sawing, hold the batten firmly against the back surface of the mitre box or of the precision mitre saw cutting box.

(3) Begin a cut by pulling the saw backwards two or three times until it slides forwards easily.

(4) Cut right to the base of the line – it is easy to finish too early and allow the timber to snap off, leaving a ragged line that will mar the joint.

(5) When possible, cut mitred pieces in opposing pairs, marking the second against the first.

(6) Sand the edges before assembling the joint.

SOLDERING

This is a useful way of joining brass and copper wire, or smaller square or round sections of the metals. The main difficulty is the problem of holding delicate components in exactly the right position by means of tools such as tweezers or small pliers: heat from the soldering iron makes it impossible to use fingers to hold the metal. A big advantage is that solder, being a metal, can fill gaps; the downside of this is the possible formation of globules of unwanted solder that have to be removed afterwards.

Similar to soldering a plumbing joint, the process is basically to clean all the parts to be joined with steel wool until they shine brightly, apply liquid or paste flux, place the items against one another, then apply the reel of wire solder at the same time as the point of the soldering iron is applied.

When cool, the joint is cleaned up with a metal file, then all traces of flux residue are washed away (this can be corrosive if left *in situ*).

PROBLEMS AND SOLUTIONS – SOLDERING

(P) Solder forms as a large bubble away from the point where it is required.

(S) Dismantle the joint, clean the components, apply more flux and try again.

(P) Lumps of solder accumulate in a place that is hard to reach with a file or hacksaw blade.

(S) Carefully re-melt the solder so that it drops away or spreads to a place where it can easily be removed.

(P) After soldering is completed, it transpires that components are fixed in the wrong place or at the wrong angle.

(S) Re-melt and try again. This very often happens, and a couple of trial runs are sometimes needed to get components lined up correctly. Once the soldered joint is melted, it will stay that way whilst the iron is against it, and for a couple of seconds after the heat source leaves. It can often be helpful to draw the intended shape of an assembly on to a board beneath the proposed joint(s), then you can line up angles and judge relative positions from above, while soldering.

(P) As solder is melted, it flows in the wrong direction.

(S) Try to use gravity so that you solder downwards wherever possible. Where this is impossible, melt a small amount of solder on to each piece separately before assembly, then apply heat to unite the two areas.

(P) It is hard to remove unwanted excess solder.

(S) Try using the blade from a junior hacksaw to cut away the piece from either side, followed by a sharp file. Remember, metal files become blunt and solder is likely to be very hard, so get one that cuts quickly.

(P) The soldering iron only works when parts of the point touch the joint.

(S) Clean the point with a file or emery paper until the metal is bright and clean.

USING GLASS-REINFORCED PLASTIC (GRP)

MAKING PANELS

Use the polyester resin and the special white matting material, which is made up of strands of glass bound together by a dissolvable adhesive, when casting a panel against a flat sheet mould.

Apply a release agent (usually PVA-based) to the mould's surface. Mix and paint on a gel coat (a special thixotropic formulation of resin) and wait for this to dry. Paint the surface of the dried material with ordinary polyester resin and lay pieces of the matting on top. Repeatedly stipple the back of the matt with a brush loaded with more resin, until it becomes translucent. Continue with more layers if required, according to desired thickness.

Overlap the edges. When dry, remove the panel from the mould and trim the edges with a metal- or plastic-cutting saw or jigsaw blade.

USING AIR-HARDENING CLAY

- Thin layers can be produced by rolling the material with a rolling pin, milk bottle, piece of large round dowelling or something similar. This can be useful if you want to apply it as a sheet, for example when replicating brickwork or paving slabs.
- A rolling pin can also be useful for smoothing out the material *in situ*.
- Since it dries in the air, the best way to prevent partly-finished work drying out is to cover it with kitchen film.
- If the surface begins to dry while you are working on it, spray it lightly with water from an atomizer.
- To make sure that clay bonds to MDF or plywood, apply a generous coating of PVA adhesive to the wood material first.
- To make grooves, such as the gaps between brick courses, use a pointed modelling tool, long nail or bodkin. The clay sometimes tends to 'pick up' at the end of a grooving stroke, leaving raised clay edges that mar the material's smoothness. If it is not possible to eradicate these rough areas at the time, sanding with medium sandpaper when the clay is dry removes them.

— 7 —

Roofs

Since Tudor roofs are generally fairly steep, it is wise to make them opening or removable, rather than wasting the space. Methods vary according to the type. Normally made from 6mm (¼in) MDF or plywood panels, supported by an internal framework, the surface of the panel is decorated with either actual dolls' house roof tiles (thin plywood cut to represent tiles), air-hardening clay, or thatch.

The highest point, the roof line, is called the ridge, often covering a ridge pole (joining the side walls of the house) and covered by ridge tiles (or thatch); the lowest points of the main panels are the eaves. Eaves normally project slightly over the front and back of the house, as do the sides. Construction of the main types of roof is dealt with first, followed by the application of tiles or thatch.

The proposed position of the chimney has to be considered, and can cause problems regarding roof hinging, if this is required.

Fig. 78 Long steep roofs, twice as high as the ground floor.

Fig. 79   Long steep roof – gable wall is at right angles to it.

MAKING MDF/PLYWOOD PANELS MEET NEATLY AT AN ANGLE

If two panels are held together at their top edges to form an angle representing that of the roof's slope, a valley will be formed where they meet. This may be acceptable, if, for instance, a piece of round dowel is to be inserted that is to be later carved to represent ridge tiles. Alternatively, to make them meet without a valley, plane down the underside edge of each until they meet in a single line. It is important to avoid planing anything from the top surface, as gaps could occur. Judge the amount of material to be removed and keep checking for accuracy.

GABLED ROOF

This is the simplest type of roof to make, and is normally created by terminating the two side walls as pointed triangles, whose apexes support the ridge of the roof.

OPENING

Total removal is possible, but the roof would be heavy for a child to lift, and the upper storey would be left without a rear

Fig. 80   Gable wall roof terminates as a gablet-style roof.

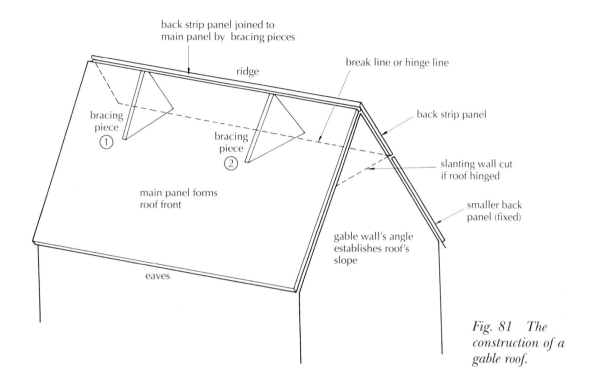

Fig. 81 The construction of a gable roof.

wall. A good alternative is to establish a line along the back roof panel, two or three inches below the ridge, and use this as a break line. The front panel, ridge part and a short part of the rear panel is thus constructed as one piece and lifts on and off, supported by the apexes of the side panels. Hinging this is also possible, but in this case it would be necessary to incorporate part of the top section of the house side within the roof part to be raised, as shown. Bear in mind also the thickness of the roofing material – two thicknesses of thatch or thick roof tile would prevent the roof from opening unless the hinge was flush with the top surface of this material. Hinging at the actual apex is also possible, but some kind of stay would be needed to keep it raised. In all these cases, the back part of the roof panel is fixed in place.

CONSTRUCTION (REMOVABLE OR HINGED)

Comprising: main front panel and shorter length to which it is attached (this hangs

Fig. 82 Joining main roof panels – a completely removable roof is being made for the project house (see Chapter 16).

over the ridge and down the back side), and either two or three triangular bracing pieces (9mm/⅜in or 12mm/½in) plywood or MDF.

Method
(1) Cut the pieces. Holding them against the house itself, decide whether to chamfer the underside of the panels or not, then perform this procedure if necessary.
(2) Cut two (or three for a long roof) support triangles of 9mm (⅜in) or 12mm (½in) plywood or MDF, their angle being the same as that of the house sides.
(3) Fit these between the two panels, checking that they hold them together at the requisite angle. It may be necessary to cut away the top corner of the support to ensure a snug fit.
(4) Screw, countersink and glue them in place (*see* Chapter 6), making sure that their position does not correspond with either of the side walls or any interior walls.

HIPPED ROOF

This is more complicated, because the four panels have to meet at different angles.

OPENING

The complete roof could be hinged at the back for the whole thing to open, or the entire roof could be made to lift off. There is no neat way of splitting this type of roof so as to allow only a part of it to open.

CONSTRUCTION

Comprising: two main panels, two end panels, bracing triangles, battening pieces.

Method
(1) Cut the main panels, beginning with a rectangle, then drawing a line marking off the main side angles and removing these.
(2) Join these together as in steps 2–4 for gable roof construction, first chamfering the top edges if required.
(3) Cut the end panels, oversized.

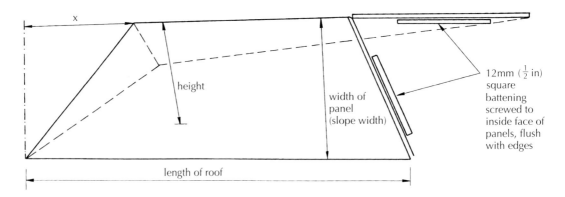

Fig. 83   The construction of a hipped roof.

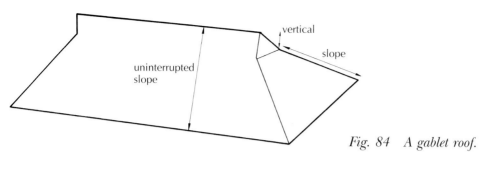

Fig. 84   A gablet roof.

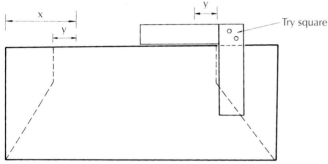

Fig. 85   Method of marking gablet roof main panels.

(4) Glue and screw short pieces of 12mm (½in) square battening, their visible surfaces flush with the panels' edges.

(5) Glue and screw (countersink) the end panels on to these batten pieces.

(6) Trim off most of the waste from the end panels using the jigsaw, following the angle of slope of the main roof. NB. Do not trim close up to the main panel – leave 3mm (⅛in) or so proud.

(7) Plane away the end panel material so that the main panel and the trimmed edge of the end panel are flush.

(8) You may find it worthwhile to have an integral base panel to fix the assembly on to (*see* Chapter 16).

GABLET ROOF

Made as a hipped roof, but the two main panels are cut as shown, the size of the right-angled corner shape determined according to taste.

CONSTRUCTION

Comprising: two main panels, two end panels and triangular right and left ridge pieces attached to the end panels.

Method
(1) Cut the main panels, beginning with a rectangle, then drawing a line marking off the main side angles.

(2) Then hold a try-square against the panel's edge, a short distance (y) beyond the end point of this line, and draw a line at right angles to the panel's edge, thus giving a right-angled top 'ear' to the ridge ends of the main panels. Cut along the marked lines.

(3) Continue as for the hipped roof, but trim off the top part of the end panels so that they fit against the main panels.

(4) Add pieces to close off the triangular holes at each end of the ridge.

MAKING DORMER WINDOWS FOR INCORPORATION INTO A MAIN PANEL OF A ROOF

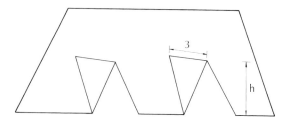

Fig. 86 Dormer window in a main roof panel.

Crucially, the top ridge part of these (they are usually paired) assemblies and the front face of the gable window must be parallel with the front of the house, with its top ridge at right angles to this, there-fore parallel with the floor lines of the house.

CONSTRUCTION

Comprising: two sides and a triangular front, this part housing a window opening.

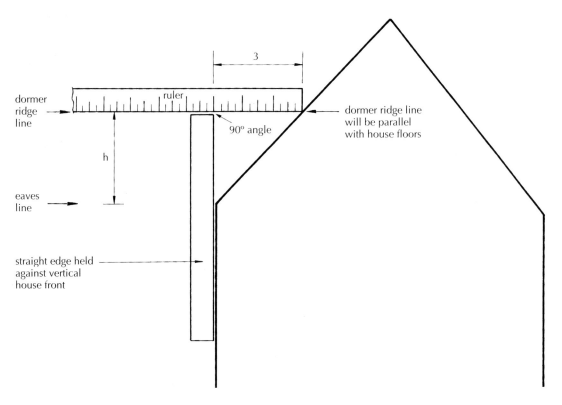

Fig. 87 Ascertaining dimensions for a dormer window.

Fig. 88   Large dormer window above front façade.

Fig. 89   Single central dormer.

Fig. 90   Dormer – its ridge is 'dropped' and curving, but still apparently waterproof.

Method

(1) With the roof in place, hold a long straight edge or length of wood against the front of the house, projecting up in front of the roof, ensuring it is parallel with the house front. Measure and mark on this the distance (h) from the eaves line.

(2) Measure the distance at the side from here to the roof, and record this (z). The two sides are therefore right-angled triangles, with one side (z), the other side (h). Mark and cut these from 6mm (¼in) MDF or plywood.

(3) Cut the front triangular window panel according to taste, making the requisite window holes.

(4) Hold the panels against the top side edges of the window panel and the roof. Plane the undersides of the panels so that they fit the roof planes neatly.

(5) Mark the position of the window panel on the roof, and cut away a piece of the roof panel to accommodate the window panel's lower edge.

(6) Use 12 × 12mm (½ × ½in) batten as joining blocks to join the side panels to the window panel and the side panels to the roof. Screw and glue the assembly together.

(7) Trim inside the roof panel to remove any material behind the window's opening.

ROOF SURFACE TREATMENTS

TILES

A principle of tiling is that the joints between tiles are staggered, row above row, meaning that each tile join should come exactly to the mid-point of a complete tile

Fig. 91   Tiled roof. Note the gentle undulations that might not be appropriate on a miniature.

Fig. 92   Hipped end of a tiled roof.

Fig. 93   Tiled roof with tile gable frontage.

in the row below, so that rainwater falling between them hits the surface of the complete tile beneath, thus keeping the roof waterproof. Building practice allows for this half-tile extra length in alternate rows by the use of larger tiles (one-and-a-half times usual width) at the end of rows, but for a dolls' house it looks perfectly acceptable to simply leave a half tile at the end.

Tiling a Roof Panel Using 0.8mm (1/32in) Plywood

Small sheets of the thin plywood are cut into strips (grain running lengthways). These strips have slits cut at regular intervals, each slit extending a little beyond half the strip's width.

(1) Begin with a piece of plywood slightly longer than the roof, with, if possible, the grain running lengthways. If unavailable, shorter length panels can be used. Cut a number of strips, 25mm (1in) wide. A marking gauge is the best method of marking. The quickest method is to plane the edge level after each cut, subsequently marking with the gauge and cutting the next. Identify the planed straight edges of the strips, as these will form the lower (necessarily straight) tile edges. The other long edges of the strips need not be straight, as these will be covered up.

(2) For each strip, mark a line 10mm (⅜in) from the straight edge (with the marking gauge). This denotes the line where an upper row of tiles will terminate – the overlap line.

(3) For *half* of the strips: mark along the straight edge at 20mm (¾in) intervals, and continue these lines across the width of the strip to slightly over halfway, using a try-square to ensure they are at right angles to the long edge.

(4) Mark the remaining strips in the same way, except for making an initial line only 10mm (⅜in) from one edge, then continuing to measure 20mm (⅞in) as usual. This corresponds with half a tile's width at one end (usually the left), allowing the tile joints to be staggered, as explained.

(5) Cut along these lines, ideally using an electric fretsaw or bandsaw, but otherwise a jigsaw. If you are using a jigsaw, hold the work securely in a vice, taking care that the vibration of the blade does not snap the fragile timber. NB. Always keep fingers behind and well away from the jigsaw's blade. Extend the cut to approximately 2mm (⅛₆in) beyond the overlap line. Hand-cutting with a junior or standard hacksaw, with the work held in a vice, is another alternative.

(6) Draw lines at 25mm (1in) intervals lengthways across the roof slope.

(7) Glue one strip on to the panel bottom (eaves), its bottom edge aligned with this. Line up the left-hand edge with that of the panel, allowing the overhang on the right.

(8) Stick the next strip (one with a 10mm/⅜in width tile slot cut at the left hand edge) partially to the panel and partially to the lower strip, its base edge aligned with the lower strip's overlap line.

(9) Continue in this way up to the ridge, using the lines marked on the panel to check that the strips are not beginning to slope in either direction – if this occurs, adjust subsequent strips to correct the imbalance.

(10) Adjust the top rows according to the chosen type of ridge, if necessary concluding with single tiles cut from the plywood.

(11) Trim off the right-hand side overlap until all strips are flush with the right-hand edge.

Making Ridge Tiles (For a Gable Roof)

The options include:

(1) Chamfering the underside of the long top edges of the panels so that they meet to form a sharp point, tiling almost up to this, and moulding ridge tiles with air-hardening clay. Fashion the clay to form a semi-circular curve along the ridge and make grooves in this to correspond to the position of tiles the same width as those of the main roof panel.

Fig. 94   Roof planes meeting at an internal angle (valley).

Fig. 95   Saddle-back tiles joining roof planes meeting at an external angle on a hipped roof.

(2) Chamfering as above (not necessarily enough to form a sharp angle at the ridge, but perhaps leaving a slight gap) and covering the ridge with L-shaped batten or half-round (semi-circular shaped) dowel. These timbers are then ridged with a saw to replicate the divisions between ridge tiles.

(3) Not chamfering the panels at all and using dowel to fill the resultant groove formed at the junction of the panels. The dowel is ridged as in step 2.

Tiles Meeting at Angles – Trimming Shapes to Fit

Where tiled roof surfaces meet at internal angles, for example when gable window roof sides join a main roof panel, simply trim tile strip ends to fit so that they meet as closely as possible at the angle. For external angles, such as where roof planes change within a hipped roof, do the same, without worrying about gaps. Use air-hardening clay to build a semi-circular outcrop, then shape this to replicate bonnet tiles (*see* page 28). Although not historically accurate, half-round ridge tiles could be fashioned from half-round dowelling, mirroring the way more modern hipped roof planes meet.

THATCHING A ROOF PANEL

Refer to Chapter 2 for a description of the true method of thatching. Thatch can be replicated using coconut fibre, which is available from dolls' house shops. The harsh strands are the right texture and colour for imitating straw.

The yealm is a bunch of thatch, and here refers to approximately 30 strands of the material, which tend to be around 150–200mm (6–8in) long. Liggers are timber poles used to retain the thatching material from above, represented by 3mm

(⅛in) diameter dowel, and spars are curved nails, represented in small scale by U-shaped nails.

Materials

- lengths of 12 × 1mm (½ × ¹⁄₃₂in) timber softwood strips
- 12mm (½in) panel pins
- PVA glue
- coconut fibre material
- 3mm (⅛in) diameter dowel

Method

(1) Draw lines horizontally along the roof panel, 25mm (1in) apart.

(2) Cut the thin battening slats to the same length as these lines (the width of the roof). Any smaller pieces left over can be joined to make a complete length.

(3) Drill 2mm (³⁄₆₄in) diameter holes at each end of these battens and also at 38mm (1½in) intervals along the length.

(4) Pin one end of a batten at the right-hand side, aligning its top edge with the first marked line above the eaves. NB. Only nail part of the way (leaving about 3mm/⅛in sticking up).

(5) Take some coconut strands, about 30, to make a yealm. Twist the bundle a couple of turns, then fold it in half, holding the bunch together at the top.

(6) Slide this underneath the batten.

(7) Repeat steps 5 and 6 for three or four more yealms, then nail through the next hole along to trap the yealms, ensuring that the matting lies flat against the panel and is not bunched up. Do not nail this second pin completely home, however you may now nail the first one completely home.

(8) Repeat along the batten, then repeat upwards along the roof, overlapping all the time.

Fig. 96   Making a thatched roof.

The ridge cap is made up of yealms laid side by side, held down by liggers (3mm/⅛in diameter dowels of wood, running the length of the roof), that are held, in turn, by U-shaped nails (spars). You may want to add additional liggers for a decorative effect.

(9) Comb the thatch, using a coarse-toothed metal comb, then trim to give an even effect.

Alternatively, use a sewing machine to sew the thatch on to fabric strips:

(1) Cut lengths of tape about 60mm (2⅜in) longer than the roof's width.

(2) Form a yealm and fold this in half, as step 5 above. Machine this on to the tape, using a large stitch.

(3) Repeat for other yealms to the end of the tape, then turn the assembly over and sew along the other side for strength.

(4) Repeat steps 2 and 3 for the other tapes.

(5) Stick the tapes on to the panel, overlapping by approximately an inch, using PVA adhesive. Hold in place using drawing pins until the glue has set if necessary.

(6) Comb the thatch, then trim off excess material.

— 8 —

Windows

The frames – either stone or timber – of mullion windows can be made from timber mouldings and carved, however the lead-work is not as simple. The patterns formed by the lead caming can be reproduced using garden mesh if the pattern is either square or diagonal. If you want a more complex caming design, use square-section brass for the frame, and brass wire, shaped and cut accordingly, soldered within this (*see* Chapter 6). Alternatively, use special black strips (available from model shops), applied directly to the acetate sheet.

A METAL WINDOW INCORPORATING A LEAD CAME DESIGN

MATERIALS

- soldering flux (type of liquid or paste used by an electrician or model-maker, *not* a plumber)

- square-section brass tube, 3mm (⅛in) side section
- brass wire
- solder wire

SPECIAL TOOLS

- soldering iron
- tweezers
- pliers
- small wire cutters
- junior hacksaw
- very small metal files

METHOD

(1) Make up a jig (*see* Chapter 4) to the size of the window, using plywood or MDF.
(2) Cut the sides of the frame and place them in the jig, ensuring that they fit against each other snugly.
(3) Using fine emery paper or steel wool,

Figs 97 and 98   Oriel windows.

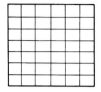

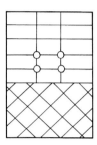
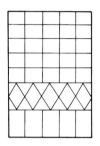

Fig. 100   Small oriel window with diamond-shaped panels.

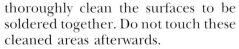

Fig. 99   Examples of different kinds of lead caming designs for windows.

Fig. 101   Oriel window with intricate lead caming designs.

Fig. 102   Oriel window with square lead caming.

thoroughly clean the surfaces to be soldered together. Do not touch these cleaned areas afterwards.

(4) Apply some flux, then melt a pool of solder on to the flat planes on the frame sides, where the ends of the end pieces are to be soldered. Solder from above.

91

Fig. 103   Mixture of diamond-shaped and rectangular-shaped lead caming.

Fig. 104   Oriel window with diamond-shaped lead caming.

Fig. 105   Close-up of window fastening handle.

Fig. 106   Close-up of window fastening bar.

(5) Place the pieces within the jig, then solder the joints.

(6) Remove the frame from the jig, turn it over and melt more solder into the joints from the underside to ensure a good bond, taking care not to disrupt the angles at which the components meet.

(7) Draw the required lead came design on a piece of card, then place the frame on top of this.

(8) Cut the brass wire to follow the shapes drawn on the card and assemble these within the frame, adjusting as necessary. Manipulating the small pieces is difficult, and tweezers may have to be used.

If circles are required, it can be helpful to wind the wire around a piece of wooden dowel, or metal drill, taking the wire beyond the circle's end. Cut through both thicknesses, and when soldered together, the resultant circle should be true. It may be necessary to squeeze the circle gently with pliers to remove any high spots.

(9) Dismantle the wire pieces and melt a small area of solder on to the inside of the frame at the points where the

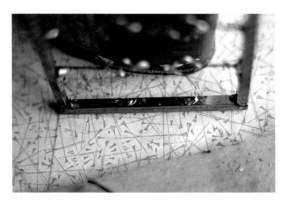

Fig. 107   Melting pools of solder on to brass strip.

Fig. 108   Winding brass wire around a drill to create a circle.

wire is to join it, first cleaning and applying flux to these areas.

(10) Reassemble the framework, apply flux, then solder the joints.

(11) Carefully file away any lumps or bumps around the joints, using a junior hacksaw blade where possible, followed by fine files.

(12) Clean with water and dry thoroughly, to remove any traces of flux.

(13) Prime, then paint the metal on both sides.

(14) Solder up another frame of the same size from either matching square-section brass, or thin flat brass strips.

(15) Cut a piece of acetate larger than the original frame and stick this on to the back of the frame using a small amount of epoxy adhesive applied to the very edges of the frame. Take care not to allow adhesive to impinge on to the see-through parts of the window. Trim away the excess acetate, so that the acetate and the metal edges are flush.

(16) Stick the frame made up in step 14 on to the back of the acetate, thus sandwiching the 'glass' between the two frames.

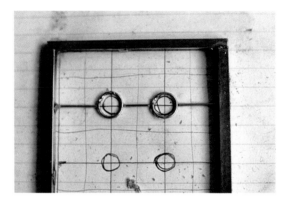

Fig. 109   Soldered joints.

As an alternative, you may prefer to stick the joints with epoxy resin adhesive rather than soldering them.

HINGING A METAL OR TIMBER WINDOW

Windows are generally too small to allow even the tiniest hinges, therefore one solution is to use tiny pins at the top and bottom, housed in the window's frame, or the front of the house.

93

(1) Drill suitable holes in the window frame and either solder, or glue with epoxy resin, short lengths of wire into the holes, leaving small pins proud of the window frame top and bottom, at the hinge side.

(2) Make a separate frame to surround the window, incorporating corresponding holes for these pins, and set the frame into the window aperture.

GLAZING (STANDARD METHOD FOR NON-OPENING WINDOWS)

(1) Make the glazing unit – the mesh alone, or the brass framework on its own or backed by the acetate – larger than the aperture by 3mm (⅛in) all around the edge.

(2) Mark an outer perimeter line 3mm (⅛in) all around the window aperture.

(3) Rebate to the depth of the glazing unit up to this line. Cut a groove with a sharp craft knife first, and remove material with a chisel.

(4) Insert the window unit, if necessary sticking it in place with contact adhesive, taking care not to let the adhesive impinge on the acetate.

(5) Stick the frame pieces and sill over the glazing unit's edge, positioning these around the aperture to cover any unsightly gaps.

RECREATING DIFFERENT TYPES OF WINDOW

STONE MULLION AND TRANSOM WINDOWS

Instead of using separate pieces to frame these, cut the entire unit from 9mm (⅜in) MDF, carving the sides of the pieces to an angle of 45 degrees. Insert the glazing units into the house façade in the usual way. Inside the house, stick battening of triangular profile on to the back of the glass for the central mullions, and picture-frame moulding angled at 45 degrees for the side, top and bottom frames.

ORIEL WINDOWS

Construct these using a combination of MDF or plywood panels and batten. The bow-shaped-type, or the curve underneath the square-type, can be replicated by using several layers of 0.8mm (½in) plywood clamped and glued together.

BOW WINDOWS

Although not strictly Tudor, their inclusion could be justified if they were assumed to have been added at a later date. Cut the top and bottom from 9mm (⅜in) MDF or plywood, and glue several layers of 0.8mm (½in) plywood around the curve. For horizontal window top frames and sills, cut the curving shapes from 9mm (⅜in) MDF or plywood, measuring the desired thickness of the frame by using dividers.

DORMER WINDOWS

Refer to Chapter 7 for instructions on making the triangular roof part above these. Otherwise, this type of window is made in the same way as the standard method, described above.

SHUTTERS

MDF of 6mm (¼in) can be carved to represent the slats of a shutter. Delineate the upper and lower edges of the slats by marking rectangular lozenges within the shutter panel. Slice a groove using a craft knife along the top horizontal lines, then make cuts at both ends of these. Use a chisel to remove the lozenge's corner to form an even slope, of approximately 45 degrees. The shutters can be hinged by inserting small tips of wire in the top and bottom of the frame and making an enclosing frame into which these slot, as for hinging windows.

Timber Framing, Pargeting and Weatherboarding

EXTERNAL BEAMS

The best method of recreating external beams is to stick battens of various sizes on to the flat panels. Generally, 12×6mm ($\frac{1}{2} \times \frac{1}{4}$in) hardwood batten suits most 1:12 scale houses, with 12×12mm ($\frac{1}{2} \times \frac{1}{2}$in) timber for window sills, and 6×6mm ($\frac{1}{4} \times \frac{1}{4}$in) for narrower parts, such as window frames, or diagonal strut pieces. Curved or circular beams can be cut from 9mm ($\frac{3}{8}$in) or 6mm ($\frac{1}{4}$in) MDF.

CUTTING TO SIZE

Measuring exactly to size and then cutting and applying is very time consuming and unnecessary. It is far better to place the batten against its desired position, mark it, then cut it there and then. A jigsaw is quickest (always keeping your non-cutting hand well away from the blade), but using a tenon or junior hacksaw guarantees more accurate results. Very often, diagonal pieces are required to join others at various angles, and the simplest accurate method is to place the batten on top of the ones it is to meet, judge the angle of junction by eye and draw across for the cuts.

SURFACE TREATMENT

Painting beams is generally much easier than staining and varnishing. For one thing, the latter treatment must be done before the beams are stuck in place, and, ideally, the panel behind should also be painted, meaning that PVA glue cannot be used – contact adhesive is the only option. A second argument against staining and varnishing is that the different types of timber used for beaming within the same project may absorb the stain at different rates, causing colour differences. More importantly, genuine Tudor timber on houses was originally left unpainted, but if subsequently left raw, it took on a silvery bleached hue. While in real life this can look beautiful, on a replica it could look bleak and unattractive. Genuine beams are either painted (black or sometimes brown) or left to accrue this silvery hue – they are not stained dark brown, and would look odd if they were. If you are using MDF for any curved beams or struts, this obviously cannot be stained.

Fig. 110   Detail of carving on a fascia board.

Fig. 111   Typical beam pattern.

STICKING BEAMS TO PANELS

PVA adhesive is excellent for bonding timber to MDF or plywood. Since the timber pieces are small and light, a good suction joint is formed immediately, and normally no kind of clamping or additional fixing is required. Use plenty of adhesive – although there may be pools of white glue apparently marring a panel's smooth appearance, these can easily be removed afterwards with a damp cloth, and if they are not they will dry clear. Occasionally it may be necessary to clamp a piece in place until the adhesive is dry, especially where long lengths are concerned. Where clamps are impractical, you may choose to drill and screw a beam to a panel as

a temporary measure. Another option, where a degree of 'grip' is required, is to use contact adhesive. Remember that if you want to stain and seal the timber, as opposed to painting it, you will need to do this before stick-ing the beams in place, and in this instance you should paint the panels first and use contact adhesive rather than PVA. Any errant strands of contact adhesive on the panels can afterwards be painted over.

FRAMING AND DIVIDING UP WINDOWS

Once the chosen type of window has been rebated into its slot, cut the upper frame piece and the sill to the exact size of the

Fig. 112   Examples of different exterior timber-beam patterns.

window and stick these in place. Then fix side-beams either side to meet their edges. If you wish to split the window into narrower panels, cut beams to be inserted vertically and fit them between the upper horizontal frame piece and the sill (accurate cutting is required). Afterwards, fit corresponding beams on the inside window frame, sandwiching the window material in between them.

ROUGHING UP EDGES AND PLANES

The neat square-cut appearance of regularly-angled timber beams is not compatible with the adze-cut coarseness of Tudor-style timber, so it is best to chamfer edges and corners with a chisel. Gouging slices from along a panel can also improve the appearance and lessen the 'clean cut' effect.

STRUTS UNDER THE JETTY

These are easily cut from 9mm (⅜in) MDF or plywood, and usually fit underneath timbers fitted directly under the jetty, that represent the ends of floor joists. If cut from plywood, and you plan to stain the timber, bear in mind that the cross-sectional view will show a sandwich of different kinds of timber, which will remain even after staining. Cutting them from fairly wide battening strips is also possible, but softwood cut to sharp curves can sometimes be fragile, and inclined to snap along the grain line. Where two struts meet at right angles, for example where a house is jettied on two sides, the two struts can be made into a dragon beam by filling the gap with air-hardening clay and shaping it accordingly (*see* Chapter 16).

PAINTING BEAMS AND PANELS

Always paint the panels first, since being of a lighter colour, any overbrushing on to the beams can easily be overpainted by the darker colour. It will be impossible to get an absolutely straight line of delineation between the two colours, but this would occur on life-size beamed houses anyway.

PARGETING

Usual pargeting designs (*see* Chapter 2) can be formed by applying textured plaster finish and marking it accordingly, but if a regular shape or pattern is required it may be worthwhile reproducing it in plaster, for which you will need to make a mould.

You first need the 'master' – either a shape or design fashioned from air-hardening clay and allowed to dry, or else an original item like a coin with a texture. NB. This method only works for small, relatively flat items, without a very deep undercut. For larger, more intricate pieces you would need special mould-making rubber.

Place a block of air-hardening clay on the table or bench. Rub washing-up liquid or Vaseline on to the face of the master, then press this, design-side down, into the block of clay. Allow the clay to harden, then remove the master. Recessed into the clay's surface should be an impression of the design, referred to as a female mould. Pour plaster of Paris, (available from a chemist, and mixed with water to the consistency of thick cream) into the mould and allow to set. When dry, remove the plaster cast. The process can be repeated as many times as required unless the mould is damaged.

Fig. 113   Close-up of beams showing ends of dowel.

Fig. 114   Close-up of carving under jetty.

Fig. 115   Carving above a door.

Fig. 116   Timber surrounding a door frame.

BRICK NOGGING

As outlined in Chapter 2, the wattle and daub infill of panels was sometimes replaced by bricks. These might be laid flat, stretcher-style, but were often laid diagonally, herringbone-style. Bricks painted contrasting colours and arranged in eye-catching patterns (diapering) can look very effective.

The brick façade would in reality finish flush (or almost flush) with the beams, so using a layer of air-hardening clay to raise the background panel's surface to this level works well. Afterwards this can be marked with a bodkin, knitting needle, bradawl or nail to represent the brick course lines and painted. Alternatively, you may prefer to mark and cut appropriate brick-line grooves in the recessed panel itself, or to do this on specially-cut thin infill panels, made from 3mm (⅛in) plywood.

WEATHERBOARDING

Use 0.8mm (¹⁄₃₂in) plywood and cut it into strips of appropriate width. Starting at the base, stick these on to the house front, overlapping by the same specific amount each time, as when using this material to tile a roof (*see* Chapter 7). If you are planning to stain and varnish the exterior, remember that PVA adhesive precludes successful wood staining, so stain the timber first. Varnishing can be done afterwards. More often, of course, genuine weatherboarding (clapboarding) was painted white or cream.

Chimneys and Chimney Stacks

The simplest method of making a stack and chimney is by attaching them to the side of a house. In reality, the stack was often inside, the chimney emerging through the roof either at one end or in the centre. This causes difficulties with the roof if it is made to open or lifts off, however, and also wastes valuable space inside the house. A solution can be to attach the chimney to the roof and forget about the stack – though illogical, this kind of pragmatic approach is perfectly acceptable. What is more, if you decide to have a chimney at or near the central part of the house, it is unlikely that you will want to take up parts of the rooms with a bulky chimney stack.

MAKING A CHIMNEY AND STACK

Use 9mm (⅜in) MDF or plywood, screwed and glued together for the sides of the structure, and 6mm (¼in) for the closing panel. The shape of the stack will be determined by the number and size of fireplaces within the house – these will project within the stack. As a rule, once above the highest fireplace, the stack narrows considerably on either side.

CREATING A BRICK FINISH

This can be replicated using air-hardening clay in the following manner, assuming the surface you are covering is MDF or plywood. (*See also* Chapter 6.)

Fig. 117   *Chimney with brick outcrop at top.*

Fig. 118   *Brick outcrop on four-sided chimney.*

Fig. 119   Air-hardening clay replicating brick chimney stack.

(1) Roll the clay on a flat board until it is approximately 3mm (⅛in) thick.

(2) Cut rectangular pieces suitable for covering the sides of the stack and chimney.

(3) With the house on its back so the front chimney-stack side is upper-most, paint the surface with PVA adhesive. Then lay the pieces of clay on top, merging the clay at the joins. Use a small cylinder such as a minia-ture paint tin to eradicate any lumps at the joins until the area is covered to a uniform depth.

(4) Repeat step 3 for the back side of the chimney and stack, with the house lying on its front.

(5) Repeat the above steps in order to cover the side (largest) area of the stack, with the house standing on its end.

(6) Smooth out any unevenness as before (with a larger cylindrical roller), and trim any surplus from the edges, where the layers of clay meet.

(7) Cover any uncovered chimney/stack surfaces in the same way.

(8) Mark parallel horizontal lines in the clay to delineate the brick courses, using a knitting needle, bodkin, bradawl or long nail. The lines should be 6mm (¼in) apart for a 1:12 scale – representing 75mm (3in). First mark lines on the house sides at regular intervals (approximately 25mm/1in) to act as guides when

Fig. 120   Outcrop pattern.

Fig. 121   Tall chimney.

marking the horizontal lines – it can be very easy to deviate from parallel and slant upwards or downwards.

(9) Mark the vertical lines approximately 19mm (¾in) apart in a stretcher-bond pattern.

(10) Paint the whole area with a greyish, or yellowish-white colour (emulsion) to represent mortar between the bricks. Once this coat is dry, paint the bricks a reddish-brown. It can be worthwhile to paint small clusters of bricks a slightly redder colour, and others a browner shade. A genuine brick wall has colour variations of this type. Use offcuts of clay to test colours.

As an alternative to air-hardening clay, you may prefer to carve the MDF or plywood surface, the grooves representing mortar between brick courses. Of the two materials, MDF is definitely the better choice for carving in this way.

PROBLEMS AND SOLUTIONS – STACK AND ROOF JUNCTURES

(P) The roof cannot be made to open or designed to be removable because of a central chimney stack.

(S) Attach the part of the chimney that is above the roof to the roof, leaving an open stack underneath. Alternatively do not have a chimney stack.

(P) The roof tiles cannot be made to fit neatly around the chimney.

(S) Tile the roof after fitting the chimney, so as to avoid gaps if possible. If gaps remain, consider using a narrow L-shaped band of air-hardening clay around the junction, painting it grey afterwards, so as to simulate lead-flashing.

(P) A chimney stack at the side prevents a gabled roof from hinging back upon itself in order to open.

(S) Make the opening roof first, hinged along the back slope, and including the top section of the gable (*see* Chapter 7) then add the chimney and stack, leaving the third side of the stack open. Slice a diagonal line across the back and front of the stack, to correspond with that of the gable wall beneath, and make sure the roof opens properly. Then add the stack's third side, and cut it across to match the cut lines below. Decorate the stack and chimney according to taste and then slice through the decorations to the cut line beneath.

CHIMNEY POTS

Since chimney pots were not used in Tudor times, their inclusion could look inappropriate on a house of that era, unless you take the view that it has been modernised since it was built. Certainly, small, inconspicuous pots would not look particularly out of place. Double or single pots can best be represented using appropriately-sized wooden dowel, or pieces of 15mm (⅝in) diameter copper plumbers' pipe. Dowel can be stuck flat on to the chimney top using PVA adhesive, but it is best to drill a hole for the copper pipe before sticking it in place with epoxy resin adhesive.

ELABORATELY BRICKED CHIMNEY TOP OUTCROPS

Very often, a chimney of square cross-section terminates with a larger box shape, either one uniform size larger or built upwards in a number of steps of increas-

9mm (⅜in)
or
6mm (¼in)
MDF or
plywood
squares
overlapping
each other

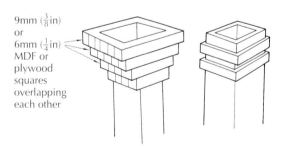

Fig. 122   Examples of different chimney tops.

ing size. You may also wish to recreate hexagonal, or other unusual shapes of chimney top (*see* Chapter 2).

Generally, these designs were made by increasing the size of the layers by half or one brick extra around the perimeter, which can easily be replicated by cutting rectangles of 6mm (¼in) MDF or plywood of a suitable size and sticking these on top of one another. Each has a central hole, and the entire structure can afterwards be 'bricked' with clay.

MAKING A SPIRAL CHIMNEY TOP

Materials
- 9mm (⅜in), or 6mm (¼in) MDF or plywood
- air-hardening clay
- 100mm (4in) nail

Method
(1) Assuming you have a square-section chimney stack, decide on a size of square slightly larger than this. As an example, in the project outlined in Chapter 16, the stack is 50×50mm (2×2in), and the larger-section size chosen was 65×65mm ($2\frac{1}{2} \times 2\frac{1}{2}$in).

(2) Cut a number of squares of the MDF or plywood to this size; 9mm (⅜in) is easiest to use, but in fact is slightly out of scale, meaning that the height of bricks would be 100mm (4in), rather than 75mm (3in). Since the builders would use differently-sized bricks within a chimney anyway, having these larger ones at the top does not matter.

(3) Drill a hole in the centre of each square, large enough to accept a 100mm (4in) nail.

(4) Set the marking gauge to approximately 4mm (⅛in) and mark this distance on the top surface of each

Fig. 123   Clamping MDF squares together to make a spiral chimney top.

Fig. 124   Spiral chimney top after clay has been added.

square, measuring from one corner.

(5) Slide the squares on to the nail, marked surfaces uppermost, then position each square above the one below, so that its edge coincides with the marked point. If the resultant 'twist' looks wrong, adjust the distance marked in step 4, dismantle the structure and re-mark the pieces.

(6) When you are satisfied with the appearance, dismantle and reassemble using PVA adhesive to stick the squares together. Spread the glue right up to the edges, not just in the centre.

(7) Once the assembly has dried, cut out its centre to make a circular hole. Use dividers to mark this, using the nail hole as a centre, then drill a series of holes of ever-increasing size around its circumference. When the holes join and the centre drops out, clean up the inside of the hole with sandpaper and/or a half-round file.

(8) Cut appropriately-sized strips of air-hardening clay, apply PVA adhesive to the edges of each square, then apply the clay. Trim any overlaps from the upper and lower edges so that the clay edges finish flush with the timber.

(9) Mark the brick lines in the clay.

(10) If necessary, carefully sand the clay surface when hardened to eradicate any unevenness.

MAKING HEXAGONAL/PENTAGONAL CHIMNEY TOPS

Cut a top and bottom piece of the required shape, then glue thin plywood (0.8mm/ ½₂in) on to the sides to represent the different facets. Add clay and groove for brickwork.

Fireplaces

A straightforward inglenook fireplace is quite simple to make. A, B and C are pieces of 6mm (¼in) or 9mm (⅜in) MDF or plywood, constructed as a three-sided box of suitable size to fit inside the throat of the chimney stack. D and E are flange pieces that are fixed to the front edges of A and B and fit across the house wall, to the left and right of the fireplace opening. These can be covered with a thin layer of air-hardening clay which is carved to represent bricks (*see* Chapter 10). Refer to Chapter 3 for details of fireplace component parts.

Above the structure is the bressumer. This can be a substantial piece of batten, part of its depth actually let into the thickness of the house wall (remember it cannot go deeper than this unless your stack is wide enough to accept it), or else a thinner batten fixed across the wall above the opening, about 6mm (¼in) thick.

It is in fact more correct to have the chimney inside the house, and this makes fireplace construction easier, so if space is not at a premium, and you do not want a chimney stack on the outside face of the house, this is well worth considering.

You may want to make a feature of a large fireplace in the central part of the house, in which case an extra wall would be required. The space need not be wasted – stairs could be incorporated (as they often were) in this 'cavity' area behind the fireplace. The inglenook itself could include bench seating.

STONE FIREPLACE

Wooden moulding can be used to represent carved stone, and can be painted grey or a honey colour. The frieze can be made from a 19 × 19mm (¾ × ¾in) central core, with a 9 × 9mm (⅜ × ⅜in) quadrant picture-frame-type moulding at the front and sides (mitred at the corners). Jambs can be made from a combination of 9 × 9mm (⅜ × ⅜in) square batten and 6mm (¼in) dowelling, to simulate curved reveals at the front. The fireback and hearth can be made from 6mm (¼in) MDF or plywood, suitably grooved to represent the joins between large slabs of stone, or covered with air-hardening clay into which brick courses are carved.

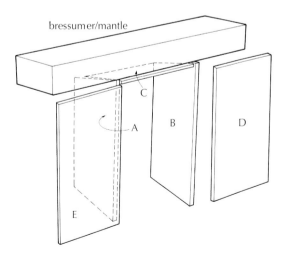

Fig. 125   Making an inglenook fireplace.

Fig. 126   Replicated fireplace.

LARGE INGLENOOK FIREPLACE WITH RECESSES IN THE SIDE WALLS

This fireplace needs an extra wide chimney stack, to allow for the various recesses. In its centre is a brick plinth for placing the grate or fire-dogs.

SMALL FIREPLACE

While not exactly Tudor, it is very likely that this kind of smaller fireplace would have been installed in an older-style house in more recent times, in an upstairs bedroom for example, and is thus in keeping with the period. Make the backing from 6mm (¼in) MDF or plywood, the lintel and jambs from suitable timber mouldings, and the hearth from MDF or ply.

BRICK FIREPLACE WITH CURVED FRIEZE

The lintel, the area above the lintel and the sides can be cut from MDF or plywood, and clay applied to the surfaces, grooved for brickwork, with the lintel bricks slightly larger and at different angles to the rest.

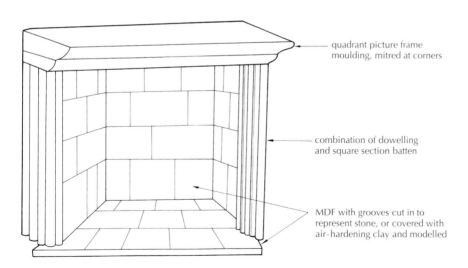

quadrant picture frame moulding, mitred at corners

combination of dowelling and square section batten

MDF with grooves cut in to represent stone, or covered with air-hardening clay and modelled

Fig. 127   Replicating a stone fireplace.

107

Fig. 128   A range of grates available from specialist dolls' house shops.

FIREPLACE ACCESSORIES

GRATE AND FIRE-DOGS

A rectangular grate can be made by soldering pieces of 5mm (³⁄₁₆in) square-section brass and flat brass strips together. It can also be made from small sections of timber, for example balsa wood. Fire-dogs can be made in a similar way. Both should be painted black, to simulate iron.

Alternatively, electric grates that simulate glowing red coals are available from dolls' house shops.

FIREBACK

This can be made from any thin material, for example 0.8mm (¹⁄₃₂in) or thicker plywood, and could be decorated in clay with designs impressed on top, if required. It should also be painted black.

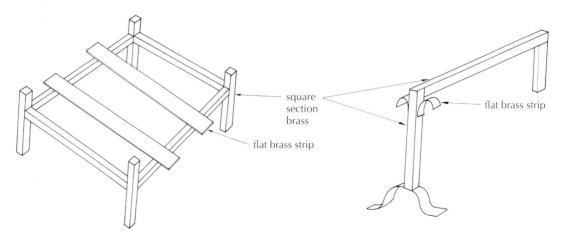

Fig. 129   Making a grate and fire-dogs.

— 12 —

Floors

FLOORBOARDS

The most straightforward kind of floor-boarding to create is close-boarded/running across the joists. While the actual building's upper-storey floor and lower-storey ceiling were often one and the same, the practicalities of making a model house mean that a piece of plywood or MDF, usually of 9mm (⅜in) thickness (or at least 6mm/¼in) will form the floor/ceiling unit, and the floorboards will either be carved into its top surface or be made up of separate thin timber strips stuck on to it. The joists are fixed underneath this panel (the ground-floor ceiling), and look most natural if they are running at right angles to the boards.

To recreate joist-and-boarded or close-boarded/parallel to joists floors would look odd with the thickness of the floor in

Fig. 130 Floorboards replicated in plywood.

between, as, for a 1:12 scale dolls' house, this would represent about 108mm (4½in), which is more the thickness of timber joists than floorboards. It is likely to look odd having floorboards running from the front to the back of the house, therefore it is most logical to remember to have the ceiling joists running from front to back, at right angles to the boards above. If at all practical, aim to have the boards meeting above a joist, as would happen in a real house (where they are nailed to this joist, which supports the ends).

CARVING FLOORBOARDS ON A PLYWOOD SURFACE

Clearly this must be done with the floor separate from the house – before final assembly. The grain of the plywood must run in the direction of the boards, that is from side to side. Decide on the width of board. For a 1:12 scale house 12–15 mm (½–⅝in) is an acceptable width, representing about 150–200mm (6–8 in). You may want to vary the widths slightly to truly mirror the less uniform widths of boards in actual Tudor houses, but be careful not to vary them too much or the effect could look false on a small scale. Decide on a suitable length of board, staggering the joints on alternate courses, bearing in mind the fact that they would have been joined over a joist. It may be impossible to arrange this in a small space, and if some boards do not meet above a joist it is unlikely to be noticed.

Fig. 131   Removing a sliver of timber for board dividing lines.

MARKING AND CUTTING FLOORBOARDS

Mark the parallel-to-grain lines along the grain to represent the separate board divisions, using an HB pencil, marking lightly. Measure from the front edge, as the depth of the room may be such as to necessitate a narrower board, which is least likely to be noticed at the rear. Then mark the cross-grain-lines – representing where boards meet.

For all parallel-grain lines: using a sharp craft knife and a metal ruler, cut a groove along the line. Move the ruler fractionally

Fig. 132   Board division lines cut for one third of panel.

Fig. 133   All lines carved.

to one side of the groove so formed and make another cut, slicing at an angle so that the blade joins the first incision.

Prise up the sliver of timber between the two cut lines, using a sharp-pointed bradawl.

For all cross-grain-lines: cut along the line, then make another cut as before, fractionally away from the first cut, but this time without angling the blade. Drag the point of a bradawl in the valley between the two grooves to remove material in between.

Afterwards, sand the surface to remove any traces of pencil lines, stain to a dark colour, and seal with polyurethane varnish.

LAYING INDIVIDUAL FLOORBOARDS

Available from specialist dolls' house shops, these are 1.5mm ($\frac{1}{16}$in) thick, 12mm ($\frac{1}{2}$in) wide strips, that are already stained. They can be fixed to floors in an assembled house (using PVA adhesive), and are usually long enough for whatever length may be required and can be trimmed with a craft knife. When laid, they simply need sealing. Extremely life-like and to scale (1:12), these are convenient to use, neat and effective.

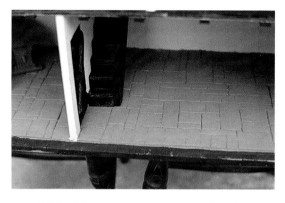

Fig. 134 Flagstone tiles reproduced using air-hardening clay.

If you have a bandsaw you may wish to cut your own floorboards from 0.8mm (½₂in) plywood, to be fixed in the same way as shop-bought ones.

FLAGSTONE FLOORS

Beautifully-produced reproduction flagstones are available, made from stone itself. These are fixed with PVA adhesive. They can be cut as required with a junior hacksaw, to fill awkward shapes and the gaps beneath door apertures. Any unevenly-sized flagstones should be positioned at the rear of the room(s).

Alternatively, you can make your own flagstones using air-hardening clay, as follows.

(1) Accurately measure the room's floor size. If fireplaces project across it, make a template to represent the clear area of the floor.

(2) Find a flat surface (tray/plywood/ MDF) that is about 13mm (½in) or larger all round than the room's floor size.

(3) Use a rolling pin to roll out air-hardening clay on this surface to a depth of approximately 4mm (³⁄₁₆in).

(5) Mark out and trim around the edges of the clay to the exact room size, ensuring the corners are right angles; alternatively trim around the template.

(6) With a knitting needle or bodkin, mark out the tiles as random rectangular (and/or square) shapes, starting from the front edge, and checking corners with the try-square to maintain right angles.

(7) 'Ageing' effects on tiles can be achieved by making very slight depressions in some with fingertips, and/or dabbing with a dry sponge or rubbing a tile with a damp finger to impart a sheen.

(8) Allow the clay to dry completely.

(9) Paint the clay with acrylic or emulsion paint. Light grey (with the addition of a tiny amount of blue) works well for a standard grey York-type stone, but a pinkish-red would be more suitable for a west country Cotswold type of stone. If in doubt about colours, look at the stone paving and walling available in garden centres for ideas.

(10) Make sure that the tile panel fits the room, trimming around the edges if necessary.

(11) Bond in position, using PVA glue painted generously on the plywood or MDF floor surface (must be unpainted) and the underside of the clay panel. Weight down the corners if necessary until the glue has set.

(12) Cavities underneath door apertures can be filled with air-hardening clay to bridge the gap between tiles in adjacent rooms.

(13) Finish with light varnish (sold by model shops) to seal the clay. It gives the surface a sheen, similar to polished stone.

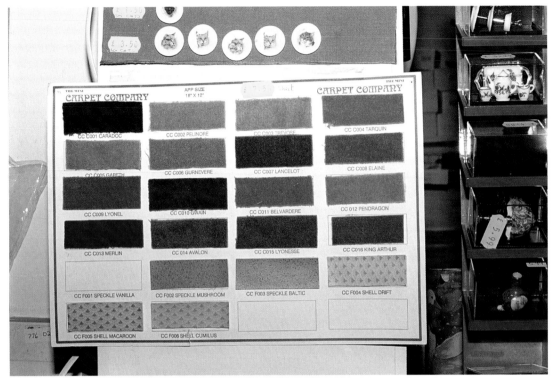

Fig. 135   Dolls' house carpets available from specialist dolls' house shops.

MARBLE

Marble-effect panels of tiles are available at dolls' house shops, and alternating coloured squares can be used to good effect.

CARPETS AND RUGS

Realistic examples are available from dolls' house shops and specialist suppliers.

Fig. 136   Dolls' house rugs available from specialist dolls' house shops.

Doors and Doorways

EXTERIOR DOORS

HEAVY TIMBER DOOR WITH A STONE SURROUND

Doors and their surrounds are inextricably linked. One idea is to fit the door behind the frame, so that the thickness of the frame can be utilised, and the edges chamfered to simulate stone.

Materials
- 6mm (¼in) MDF and 9mm (⅜in) plywood
- tiny black or brass-finish pins
- small curtain ring

Method
(1) Cut the 'stone' door frame, with a suitably-curved arch, from 6mm (¼in) MDF. Make the cut-out slightly smaller than the size of the door, so that the frame can overlap it. Plywood is not really suitable, as chamfering the edges would leave a coarse, uneven surface.

(2) Chamfer the edges surrounding the door to the required angle using a sharp chisel and sandpaper. Take care not to flatten the raised central ridge of the arch at this stage.

(3) Make the door from 9mm (⅜in) plywood (assuming the thickness of your house wall is 9mm/⅜in). It should be rectangular, not arched, thus larger than the door-frame cut-out.

(4) Cut a hole in the house front in the required position, the same size as the door.

(5) Hang the door inside this hole, making it open inwards.

(6) Remove the door and cut grooves to represent lines between boards (as for floorboard grooving, *see* Chapter 11), then stain and varnish the timber, or paint it black, according to taste. Make sure that the grooves divide the width up equally, otherwise the door will look unbalanced.

(7) Add tiny black nails to imitate the 'studding'. If only brass nails are available, partially knock them in, paint them gloss black, then knock them home fully, shielding the newly painted surface with a thin piece of wood.

(8) Use a small black-painted curtain ring fixed to a curtain eye screwed to the door to replicate the handle.

(9) Re-hang the door in its frame.

(10) Stick the door surround in front of the door, overlapping it equally all round; use the partially-covered boards at either side to judge that the overlap is equal on both sides.

(11) Glue the door jambs and lintel in place on top of the door surround. Again, be sure to centralise the lintel so that the central (highest point) of the arch is halfway along the lintel.

(12) Paint the door surround to simulate stone.

DOUBLE DOORS

Use a similar method to the above, but incorporate double doors within the surround. It can be helpful to add a narrow strip on to the front face of one of the doors where they meet, so that this bridges any gap there might be.

INTERIOR DOORS

BATTEN DOOR

Materials
- 9mm (⅜in) plywood (grain running lengthways)
- 12 × 6mm (½ × ¼in) battening
- 6mm (¼in) dowel

Method
(1) Cut vertical grooves at 12mm (½in) intervals on both sides of the door, in the same way as when carving floorboards (*see* Chapter 12).
(2) Stain the battening, unless you plan to paint the door black.
(3) Stick four lengths of 12 × 6mm (½ × ¼in) battening across the width of the door on one side. One of the battens should be near the top, another near the bottom, with the last two dividing the remaining area equally.
(4) Add some diagonal 12 × 6mm (½ × ¼in) battens between the horizontal battens, first cutting the ends of these to suitable angles to fit.
(5) Fix tiny black (or black-painted) nails into the battens to form an attractive pattern.
(6) Chamfer the batten edges so that the timber is not noticeably square cut and smooth, as for external timber beaming (*see* Chapter 9).
(7) Cut two, 25mm (1in) lengths of 6mm (¼in) dowel and stick these on the inside and the outside of the door to represent handles.
(8) Varnish the completed assembly.
(9) Instead of using 9mm (⅜in) plywood, you may prefer to stick lengths of 9mm (⅜in) square-section batten together, in which case there should be no need to make grooves, as, if the wood is stained and varnished, the divisions should be evident.

PANELLED DOOR

Cut suitable pieces of 0.8mm (½in) plywood to stick on to the door in the desired position.

Fig. 137 Exterior door – Tudor-style.

Fig. 138 A typical interior door.

Fig. 139   Exterior door and frames – Tudor-style.

VERTICAL RIBS

Vertical ribs added to any door can look impressive. Use 6mm (¼in) square-section batten, afterwards chamfering edges and corners.

HINGING

Refer to Chapter 6 for the method of rebating hinges in the edge of doors and for hanging doors. Instead of using tiny hinges, you may prefer to use cloth or special plastic hinging material (available from model shops). Sandwich the hinging material between door components and either stick it to walls, or sandwich it between walls and door surround.

Fig. 140   What was once a double door entry. Note the tilt of the door frame over time.

14

Wall Panelling and Ceiling-Beams

PANELLING A WALL

Either plywood or MDF can be used for the panels, but bear in mind that most plywood cannot be carved successfully at its edges – its cross-section is normally uneven due to the multi-layered method of production. Very high-quality plywood remains smooth in cross- section, but the different-coloured layers might absorb wood stain at different rates, marring the finish. On the other hand, plywood can be dyed successfully, and display impressive grain effects.

MDF can be shaved and carved neatly but will never show wood-grain, although staining with dark wood colours can give the appearance of timber.

In view of the above, plywood is the best material to use if you plan to stain and varnish your wainscoting, so any carving is best avoided (it is not usually necessary anyway). But if you plan to paint the timber panelling black, MDF would be an ideal choice, and panels can easily be carved to good effect.

MATERIALS

- sheet material – 3mm (⅛in) (or thinner) plywood or MDF
- quadrant moulding (if a dado rail is required)
- 12mm (½in) wide 'skirting board'-type timber strips, 1.5mm (¹⁄₁₆in) thick.

METHOD

(1) Decide on a height at which the panelling should finish – usually just above door height. Mark this around the room. You may prefer to panel the walls from floor to ceiling, in which case ignore this step.

(2) Using the sheet material specified, cut the panels to this height, or full height if step 1 is ignored, cutting around doors and windows as necessary. Start with the wall facing you, then line the walls to the right and left by butting these panels against the first. Draw pencil lines on the back panel to mark where the edges of the side walls are.

(3) Remove the panels and mark them on the back for reassembly.

(4) Mark a line from the top to indicate where the quadrant beading's lower edge will be.

(5) Stain all timber to an appropriately dark shade.

(6) For plank and muntin panelling, stick pieces of thin timber strip, the kind sold in model shops for skirting boards, on to the panels at regular intervals. Stick a horizontal plank at the bottom first, and assemble the rest between the top edge of this and the marked line at the top.

(7) For raised field panelling, either cut holes in another panel of appropriate size and stick this 'framework' panel

over the other, or stick horizontal and vertical 'skirting board' battens (as used in step 6) on to the panel, butt-jointing these against each other, and cutting the joints as close as possible. Make sure you do not encroach beyond the marked lines on the back wall panel.

(8) Stick the panels on to the walls, using contact adhesive.

(9) Glue the quadrant beading in place at the top of the panels, mitring corners as necessary.

(10) Varnish the woodwork.

RAISED FIELD PANELLING

As explained in Chapter 3, the panels within this type of wall covering have a raised central area, because all four edges slope away from this point. To carve this in MDF, mark this central lozenge, then make a deep groove with a craft knife along the outer edges. Using a sharp chisel, trim away the edges, to an angle, between the two lines only. NB. Avoid cutting beyond the marked 'raised lozenge' lines, as this would destroy the symmetry of the panel as a whole.

If you are using plywood, another idea is to use 0.8mm ($\frac{1}{32}$in) plywood to make separate lozenges fit within the framework. Sand the four side edges to replicate the bevel, stain the lozenges, then stick them in place.

LINENFOLD PANELLING

This is hard to create successfully. Use a small curved-blade chisel to shape the inner and outer vertical curves. Practise first, before tackling the panel itself. As with raised field panelling, these carved areas are set within a framework, which is raised from the main wall surface.

Fig. 141   Ceiling-beams in a Tudor cottage.

CEILING-BEAMS

Floorboards rest on floor joists, and these joists themselves rest on beams. The joists are set at right angles to the boards, and are jointed at right angles into the beams.

19 × 9mm ($\frac{3}{4} \times \frac{3}{8}$in) batten is a suitable size for beams, and 12 × 6mm ($\frac{1}{2} \times \frac{1}{4}$in) for joists. Space the joists at convenient intervals, remembering to cut them short for stairwells. Where joists cross the beams, rebate the beams out to accept the joists, using the same technique as for rebating hinges (*see* Chapter 6).

TIPS FOR BEAMING

Fig. 142   Ceiling-beams meeting at a corner.

117

Fig. 143   Replicated ceiling-beams.

- Consider the position of walls beneath the timbers, and make sure that a suitable gap is left for these, to allow the wall to fit up against the ceiling.
- Make and affix timber ceiling beams before the house is finally assembled.
- Paint beams before fixing to the (painted) ceiling.
- Remember to paint the ends of beams or joists where they abut an open stairwell.
- Nail the beams in place with tiny brass pins, ensuring these are short enough not to puncture the ceiling completely and emerge on the floor above. This is a way of avoiding the danger of adhesive staining new paintwork.
- Chamfer the beams after they are fixed in place, then touch up the paintwork

of these newly-bared areas and the nail heads (see below).

CHAMFERING BEAMS AND JOISTS

Extra authenticity can be achieved by chamfering the square edges of beams and joists, and the best method is to use a small sharp chisel. Where beams met a wall, their chamfer was sometimes completed by a 'stop' (*see* Chapter 3). You may wish to replicate such a feature before doing the main chamfering, by running a very shallow saw line a short distance from the end, and trimming the 'stop' from the corner to this line, afterwards completing the chamfer from the cut line in the normal way. Take care not to cut the line too deeply – just a few backward draws of a fine-toothed tenon, or junior hacksaw are all that are needed.

MOULDED BEAMS AND JOISTS

You may be able to find suitable timber mouldings to represent these. If you cannot, it may be possible to use several pieces of thin dowelling, stuck together. Problems occur where joists meet beams at right angles, and one solution might be to butt-joint the timbers as closely as possible and fill in the inevitable gaps with air-hardening clay, smoothed to shape to match the rest. This would naturally preclude a stained and varnished timber finish, a paint finish being the only option.

15

Stairs

Thinking of a staircase as a complete solid triangle makes all calculations simpler, as only two dimensions need to be considered: the distance from the top of the floor's surface to the ceiling, that is the height, and the available distance along the floor, the length. When considering length, remember to allow room at the top and bottom for access, and the opening span of doors.

Another factor to consider is the size of the timber for the treads. For a 1:12 house, 19mm (¾in) makes a reasonable size of tread height, working out at about 230mm (9in).

TYPES OF STAIRCASE

- Conventional – use square-section batten blocks as treads, with plywood on one or both sides, trimmed to shape.

Fig. 144 A genuine Tudor staircase.

- Triangular-section batten fitted against a flat panel – a quick and easy method of construction.
- Ladder-type, open-tread stairs – suitable for early Tudor dwellings. Made with thin slats of timber, glued to notched timber either side (strings).
- Spiral (winding) – these normally revolve around a central pole, or newel post, and can be constructed using 19 × 19mm (¾ × ¾in) section hardwood blocks, overlapping each other.

SPACE

For a large house, you may decide to break a single run in two, having one or two right-angled bends (doglegs). Another idea might be to have a minstrel's gallery above an entrance hall – an upper storey reached by a staircase, fenced off from the floor below by rails, but visible on all three sides.

As outlined in Chapter 3, Tudor staircases were actually cramped and small, often tucked away behind fireplaces, and strictly utilitarian. Existing Tudor homes usually have more conventional styles of staircase, often as a result of adding a second floor at a later date.

A straight run staircase is liable to take up approximately 180mm (7in) – representing about 2140mm (7ft) – which is hardly realistic, but even though this size would be too small in real life, any larger in the scaled-down size would take up a disproportionate amount of floor space in a dolls' house hall.

Above the staircase, a slot must be cut from the upper floor to allow for the top of the assembly leading out, and to allow access for the stair-climber's head, so that he/she does not have to duck. If you judge the slot to begin directly above the third or fourth stair, this should be adequate.

Spiral staircases can be crammed into a corner, and are ideal where space is short. All that is required is a circular (or square) hole cut in the upper floor.

COMPONENT PARTS

TREADS AND RISERS

A real staircase has separate thin planks for the horizontal treads and vertical risers, these being slotted into the side panel(s) (string(s)). For replication in miniature, both can be made from square-section 19 × 19mm (¾ × ¾in) hardwood, the length dictated by the desired width of the staircase. It is vital to cut these exactly the same size and precisely at right angles, for which a mitre block, or better still a precision mitre saw should be used. Sawing freehand will not produce right angles, meaning that the staircase cannot be assembled.

STRING

This is the side panel of the assembly. The outer string is the panel that you see covering the sides of the treads and risers, whilst the inner string is against the wall. It is usually unnecessary to include an inner string for dolls' house staircases. Plywood of 6mm (¼in) is a good choice for this if you intend to stain and varnish the staircase, or 6mm (¼in) MDF would be fine for a staircase that is to be painted.

HANDRAIL

In dwellings of later periods, staircase handrails were rounded and smooth, but medieval and Tudor types consisted of plainer, straight joists, which were strictly utilitarian and acted as a means of joining lower and upper newel posts. Either 6mm (¼in), or 12mm (½in) dowel, or 6mm (¼in) or 4mm (³⁄₁₆in) square-section battens can be used to good effect. If the square-section-type is chosen, this can be carved and etched to simulate the Tudor style.

NEWEL POST

Originally referring to the central pole around which treads were placed in a spiral staircase, this is now a more general term for the vertically-placed posts at the top, bottom and any turning point in stair runs. Tudor posts were usually made of large square timber, but later types were turned on a lathe, to make intricately-shaped part-cylindrical/part-square examples. As a rule, 12 × 12mm (½ × ½in) hardwood is a suitable size for these, and can be carved to replicate Tudor styles.

BALUSTERS

These are vertical rails joining treads to the underside of the handrail. They are not usually found in genuine Tudor staircases, but are acceptable if it is assumed that the staircase was added at a later date. Either 4mm (³⁄₁₆in) square-sided batten, or 3mm (⅛in) or 6mm (¼in) dowel could be used.

SOLID BALUSTERS

You may prefer to incorporate a baluster rail with the string, as one complete panel.

Fig. 145   A replicated staircase.

To do so, fix a larger panel to the whole assembly, mark the height of the handrail above the stairs and trim off above the line.

MAKING A STANDARD STRAIGHT RUN STAIRCASE

Comprising: 4mm (³⁄₁₆in) square batten handrail, 12mm/½in square batten for straight newel posts, 19mm (³⁄₄in) square batten for treads/risers, and 6mm (¼in) plywood for the open string.

ESTABLISHING THE STAIR LINE ON THE STRING PANEL

(1) Mark the length of stairs (l) and their height (h) on a piece of 6mm (¼in) plywood.
(2) Cut two treads/risers, the length to be the overall width of the stairs, minus 6mm (¼in) (thickness of the string). (If you plan to have a string on both sides of the treads, deduct 12mm/½in.)
(3) Place these as shown on Fig. 146, and draw the stair line from the top front

corner of the bottom tread to the top front corner of the top tread. The leading corners of the treads/risers should all follow this line.

GLUING TREADS TO THE STRING PANEL

(1) Divide the overall height by 19mm (³⁄₄in) to give you the number of steps required (rounding the figure up), and cut these, minus the two you have already cut.
(2) Apply woodstain, but not varnish, to the components and allow to dry before proceeding. Gluing the assembly together before applying the stain would mean uneven, patchy absorption because the PVA glue forms a seal, preventing stain penetration.
(3) Use PVA adhesive to glue the treads in place, keeping the horizontal treads in line with the base and making sure that the leading stair edge corners are on the stair line. In addition to applying glue to the ends of the treads/risers and the plywood face, also apply it to the parts of the blocks where they overlap, so that they are bonded together here as well. Make the overlaps as even as possible.
(4) If you are fixing a string on to both sides of the treads, glue a suitable piece of stained plywood (or plain MDF) on to the 'open' side of the stairs – the ends of the blocks.

TRIMMING WASTE AND ATTACHING NEWEL POSTS AND HANDRAIL

(1) Cut away the excess plywood. Trim the tread and riser side flush with these, but cut the underside off in a straight line, slightly below the underside corners of the stairs. You

121

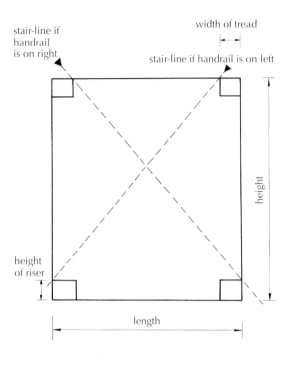

stair-line if
handrail
is on right

width of tread

stair-line if handrail is on left

height

height
of riser

length

Fig. 146   Establishing the stair line on the string panel.

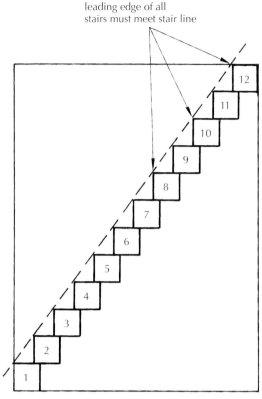

leading edge of all
stairs must meet stair line

Fig. 147   Gluing treads to the string panel.

may want to add a piece of plywood to the underside of the stairs, in which case leave enough of the string to cover its edge.

(2) Position the stairs inside the house and cut away any material from the top stair if necessary, so that they fit neatly.

(3) Cut the two newel posts so that they are long enough to fit against the side of the stair assembly, with a distance of approximately 90mm (3½in) above their respective treads. Cut a handrail, oversized. Carve these timbers according to taste, then stain them and allow them to dry.

(4) Cut angles from the side at the top and bottom of the stairs to the size of the newel posts.

(5) Drill holes on the inside faces of the newel posts to receive the ends of the handrail.

(6) Glue the newel posts and handrail in position, clamping if necessary.

N.B. If balusters are required, holes should be drilled in the underside of the handrail and the stair edges to accept these before assembly.

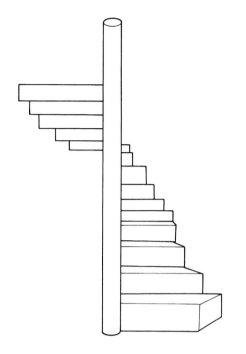

Diagram 148   Spiral staircase construction.

MAKING A TRIANGULAR BLOCK STAIRCASE

Using triangular batten, this can be mounted on two stretchers, whose bases are trimmed to match the angle of the lower floor.

MAKING A SPIRAL STAIRCASE

This is best built *in situ*, using 19mm (¾in) square batten blocks, overlapping and mounted one upon the other, and a central 6mm (¼in) or 9mm (⅜in) dowel newel post. Chamfer the corner of the blocks so that they meet the rail neatly.

PROBLEMS

TURNING CORNERS

Creating a landing or half-landing of plywood or MDF can save space and create an interesting focal point to a hallway or landing. The upper section of stairway is likely to show the underside of the treads, so in this instance they will have to be decorated in the same way as the upper sides.

MISTAKES

It is easy to miscalculate stair positions – particularly when cutting slots for the upper exit point. If you find you have removed too much floor material, you can splice in a fillet easily if you are using MDF. Just cut a close-fitting piece for the hole and glue it in place, clamping it if necessary. Afterwards, fill any gaps or depressions with fine filler and smooth to a flat surface (both sides). For plywood that has been carved and grooved to represent floorboards, trim out beyond the mistake to a floorboard groove, then slice in new matching material, making sure that its surface is slightly proud of the top (carved and grooved) surface. When it is dry, sand away material and carve and groove the new fillet to match the rest. Fill the depression underneath (the ceiling of the room below) with fine filler, then sand flush with the rest.

FIXING TO THE WALL

This can sometimes be awkward. Using contact adhesive is likely to mess up any decoration, so the best way is to mark the position of a couple of treads on the wall and drill screw holes, to mount the stairs in this way. A very small, short-handled screwdriver is likely to be required.

123

Project – Making a 'Wealden'-Style House

EXTERIOR

The Crowood is a Wealden-style house with intricate timber framing, jettying at the front and sides, and a gablet roof that overlaps all round. The house is front opening, and the split is approximately a third of the way along from the right; the right

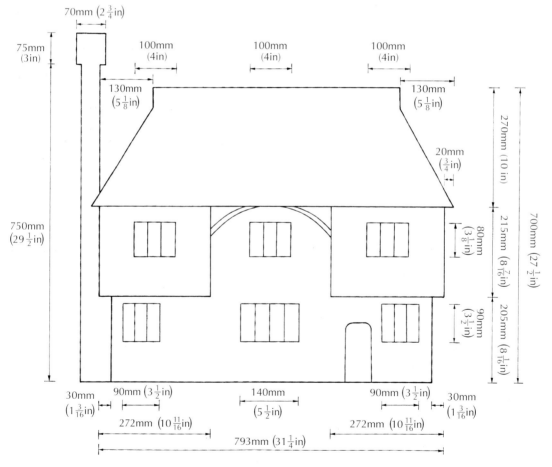

Fig. 149   Front elevation showing general dimensions.

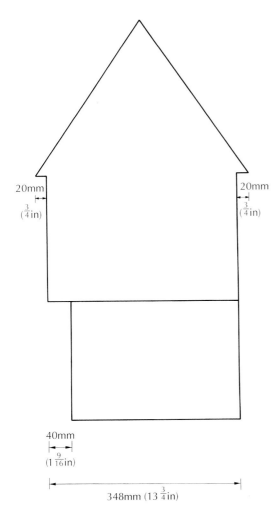

20mm
$\frac{3}{4}$in)

20mm
($\frac{3}{4}$in)

40mm
($1\frac{9}{16}$in)

348mm (13$\frac{3}{4}$in)

Fig. 150   Side elevation showing general dimensions.

panel overlaps the left (larger) panel. The roof is totally removable for access to the three attic rooms.

There is a single large brick chimney and stack attached to the left-hand side of the house, with a spiralled, brick chimney top. The yellow of the panels juxtaposed with the dark brown timbers may not be everyone's choice: black beams and white panels, or brown beams and cream panels, or some other colour combination may be preferred. Similarly with the roof: a dark red with darker patches was decided on, but there are many other alternatives.

The roof is tiled using the thin plywood method (*see* Chapter 7), with the sloping hip faces of the roof joined to each other with simulated saddle-back tiles, made with air-hardening clay, as is the ridge. The gablet style of roof – hipped with small 'upright' sections at the eaves – is a typical Wealden-style, but you may prefer a straightforward gable roof, in which case additional side sections should be added to the upper storey, and the roof altered accordingly. Or you may prefer a straightforward hipped roof, which requires only minor modifications to the plans.

The windows are timber-framed with 12 × 6mm (½ × ¼in) batten, and 12 × 12mm (½in × ½in) sill, and made from acetate, with garden mesh (6mm/¼in) applied on top to make a diamond pattern. You may want to make more intricate simulated lead-work designs for some or all of the windows, in which case refer to Chapter 8.

INTERIOR

The ground floor has two large rooms to the right and left, and another in the middle, housing the staircase. The first floor (also with three rooms) has stairs in the central room, which is a smaller, landing-type area. On the attic floor, the stairs lead out into the centre of the central room rather than against a wall, and you may wish to add a guard rail around this. It would be quite simple to utilise a spiral staircase for access to one or both of the upper rooms, and this would ideally be situated in the far left-hand corner.

The ground-floor left-hand room has an inglenook fireplace on the left-hand wall, with a brick surface simulated from air-hardening clay. You may wish to add another fireplace in the left-hand first-floor room since it abuts the chimney stack outside, but if so, adapt the stack dimensions to make sure that the depth of your chosen fireplace fits inside it.

The ground floor is finished with simulated flagstones (air-hardening clay, painted grey), the first floor with plywood carved to represent floorboards, and the attic floor is made of MDF, and has ready-made floorboards (from a specialist dolls' house shop) bonded to it, to show the effects of the two types of floorboard within one house. It is more likely that you will prefer to choose just one effect for the sake of continuity. But of course Tudor house-builders might easily have made different floors in the same house from different sizes or types of timber.

Interior walls are painted white, as are the ceilings. Details of beamed ceilings are shown for the other pictured house (see below), from which the effect can be judged when deciding whether to do the same. You may also want to add wainscoting to the lower parts of the walls, in which case refer to Chapter 14.

Doors have plank and muntin panelling, and Chapter 13 gives details of their construction. Dark timber architraves would enhance the appearance of the doors.

DIMENSIONS OF THE HOUSE

Width: 890mm (35⅛in) at widest point.
Depth: 400mm (15⅞in) (including roof overhang); 350mm (13¾in) for just the main house depth, not including roof overhang.
Height: 710mm (28in) to apex of roof; 820mm (32¼in) to top of chimney.

SIZE OF ROOMS

Ground Floor
Depth: 280mm(11⅛in); Height floor-to-ceiling: 197mm (7¾in)
Left-hand room width: 243mm (9⅝in)
Middle room width 202mm (8in)
Right-hand room width 245mm (9⅝in)

First Floor
Depth: 280mm(11⅛in); Height floor-to-ceiling: 196mm (7¾in)
Left-hand room width: 310mm(12⅛in)
Middle room width: 170mm (6¾in)
Right-hand room width: 275mm (10⅞in)

Top (Attic) Floor
Depth: 335mm(13⅛in); Height floor-to-roof apex: 260mm (10¼in)
Left-hand room width: 235mm (9¼in)
Middle room width: 304mm (12in)
Right-hand room width: 235mm (9¼in)

TOOLS

FOR MEASURING AND MARKING

- marking gauge
- bevel gauge
- try square
- pencils: 2H and HB
- large measuring rule (1m/39in), straight enough to act as a straight edge
- straight edge, if rule is unsuitable
- medium-sized measuring rule (300mm/12in)
- small measuring rule (150mm/6in)
- retractable metal tape-measure
- bradawl with sharp point.

GENERAL TOOLS

- jigsaw with fine-wood cutting blades
- electric hand drill with high-speed steel

twist bits: 2mm (5/64in), 3mm (1/8in), 6mm (1/4in), plus countersink bit
- junior hacksaw
- fine-toothed tenon saw, or precision mitre saw, for cutting battens
- small Phillips or Pozidrive screwdriver
- small, and very small, ordinary screwdrivers
- jack plane plus, ideally, smaller plane
- chisels: 6mm (1/4in) and 13mm (1/2in)
- paint brushes: 50mm (2in), 25mm (1in) and 6mm (1/4in), plus tiny artist's brush for intricate work
- small craft knife and blades
- oilstone and oil
- vice with wooden jaw inserts
- table or workbench
- four G-clamps: 150mm (6in) or larger
- bodkin or knitting needle for marking lines on air-hardening clay

MATERIALS

All materials are shown with metric and imperial sizes. Whichever unit of measurement you choose, stick to it throughout, as mixing the two will create errors. MDF was used for most of the structure, (apart from the first floor), but plywood could be substituted, as long as the grain is filled before painting with fine surface-filler.

9mm (3/8in) MDF

Back
793 × 420mm (31¼ × 16 9/16in)
Ground floor
715 × 280mm (28 3/16 × 11in)
Top floor
793 × 335mm (31¼ × 13⅛in)
First-floor sides, left and right
Two 280 × 196mm (11 × 7¾in)
Ground-floor sides, left and right
Two 289 × 205mm (11⅜ × 8⅛in)

Fig. 151 Component panels.

Ground-floor walls
Two 280 × 197mm (11 × 7¾in)
First-floor walls
Two 280 × 196mm (11 × 7¾in)
Attic-floor walls
Two 335 × 265mm (13⅛ × 10½in)

Opening Front Sections

Front section left (FSL) – main panel
560 × 410mm (22⅛ × 16⅛in)
Front section right (FSR) – main panel
410 × 285mm (16⅛ × 11¼in)
FSR. Strips (width 34mm/1⅜in)
2 × 263mm (10⅜in)
2 × 187mm (7⅜in)
FSL. Top strip
530 × 40mm (20⅞ × 1⅝in)
Strips (width 34mm/1⅜in)
273mm (10¾in)
2 × 187mm (7⅜in)
196 × 40mm (7¾ × 1⅝in)

Chimney

House stack panels, front and back
Two × 280 × 75mm (11 × 3in)
Main stack sides
Two × 510 × 45mm (20⅛ × 1¾in)
Filler piece
410 × 32mm (16¼ × 1¼in)

Sloping filler pieces
Two 75 × 45mm (3 × 1¾in)

Roof
Joining blocks for main panels
Two 230 × 140mm (9 × 5½in)

6mm (¼in) MDF

Roof
Main roof panels
Two 860 × 330mm (33⅞ × 13in)
Base
860 × 450mm (33⅞ × 17¾in)
Hipped roof end panels,
left and right side
Two 430 × 280mm (17 × 11¼in)
Closers
Two 100 × 80mm (4 × 3¼in)

Opening Front Panels
FSL, front plate
273 × 205mm (10¾ × 8⅛in)
FSR, front plate
263 × 205mm (10⅜ × 8⅛in)
Strips for FSR and FSL
window rebate infills
Four 145 × 34mm (5¾ × 1⅜in)
Four 80 × 34mm (3⅛ × 1⅜in)

Chimney
Main side panel for stack
780 × 145mm (30¾ × 5¾in)

9mm (⅜in) PLYWOOD
First floor (grain lengthways)
793 × 280mm (31¼ × 11in)
Internal doors (grain widthways)
Six 150 × 65mm (6 × 2⁹⁄₁₆in)
Front door (grain widthways)
150 × 70mm (6 × 2¾in)
Staircase sides
Two 220 × 200mm (8¾ × 7⅞in)

0.8mm (¹⁄₃₂in) PLYWOOD
For roof tiling
Five 900 × 305mm (36 × 12in)
(or equivalent in smaller sheets if
larger size unavailable)

TIMBER MOULDINGS

Main uses – window frames and general
timber-beam work.

6 × 6mm (¼ × ¼in)
approximately 1830mm (6ft)
12 × 6mm (½ × ¼in)
approximately 9 × 1830mm (6ft)
12 × 12mm (½ × ½in)
approximately 1830mm (6ft)
6mm (¼in) dowel
approximately 915mm (3ft)

Plus any moulding required for extras such
as beaming ceilings or wainscoting, not
included in this project.

HARDWARE

200 × 25mm (1in) No.4 chipboard-thread
countersunk galvanised steel screws,
with Pozidrive/Phillips heads.
100 × 19mm (¾in) No.4 chipboard-thread
countersunk galvanised steel screws,
with Pozidrive/Phillips heads.
4 × 38mm (1½in) brass hinges plus brass
screws, for front opening sections.
14 × 13mm (½in) brass hinges plus brass
screws, for doors.
1 sheet of metal garden mesh for
windows, mesh size 6mm (¼in).

SUNDRIES

- PVA wood glue
- clear contact adhesive
- epoxy resin adhesive

- air-hardening clay
- wood primer paint
- metal primer paint
- emulsion paint for exterior timbers – brown on prototype
- emulsion paint for interior – white on prototype
- emulsion paint for exterior panels – dark yellow on prototype
- dark-oak wood stain – ideally spirit-based, as this is non-warping
- polyurethane wood varnish
- sandpaper – coarse, medium and fine

CONSTRUCTION

The assembly is screwed and glued together, which means that it can initially be constructed entirely without glue, using only screws, then disassembled so that the interior paintwork can be completed, after which it is finally stuck and screwed. The external beam-work, air-hardening clay bricks of the chimney and so on, can then be completed.

NB On all diagrams, where screw lines are shown close to the edge of a panel, the distance from the edge is always 4.5mm (³⁄₁₆in), running parallel to the edge; this distance corresponds to half the panel's thickness.

BACK AND FLOOR ASSEMBLY

Using: back, top floor, first floor, ground floor.

Method
(1) Cut the back panel to size. Cut holes for the stairs in the first and top floors.
(2) Mark screw lines on the back panel, then drill 2mm (³⁄₃₂in) holes along these at approximately 75mm (3in) centres. NB Mark and drill from the *inside* face of the panel to ensure maximum accuracy in construction.
(3) Mark and drill screw lines on the ground floor, first floor and top floor.
(4) Hold the ground floor in position and, using the bradawl, mark a screw destination hole in the edge of the floor, passing the bradawl through a screw host hole in the back panel, as described in Chapter 6. Make sure that

Fig. 152 Back and floor assembly.

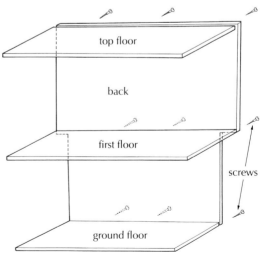

Fig. 153 Back and floor assembly.

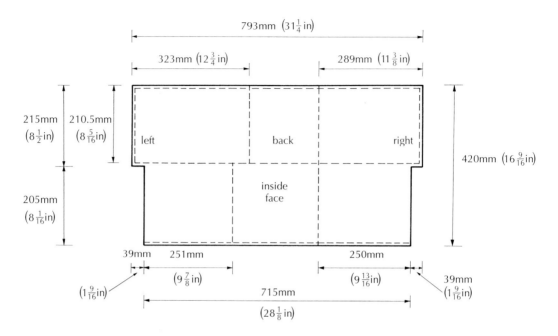

Fig. 154   Back panel, to indicate where it should be cut, and screw lines.

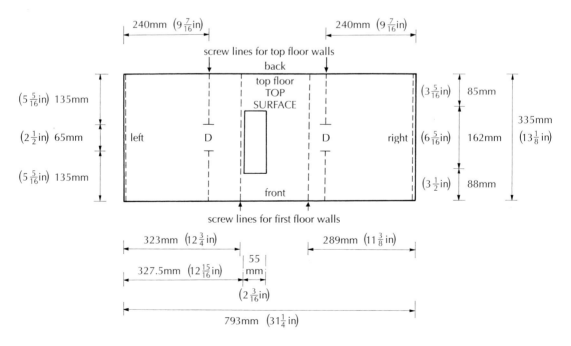

Fig. 155   Top floor (top surface), to show stairwell cut-out area and screw lines.

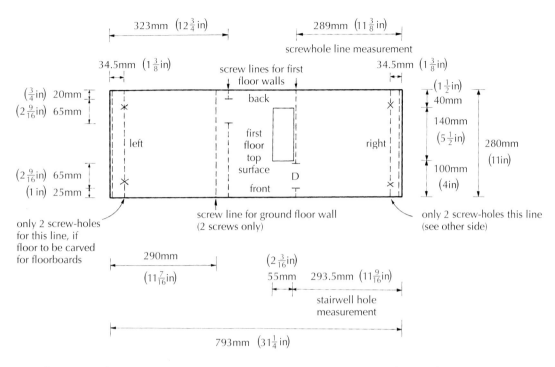

Fig. 156   First floor (top surface), to show stairwell cut-out area and screw lines.

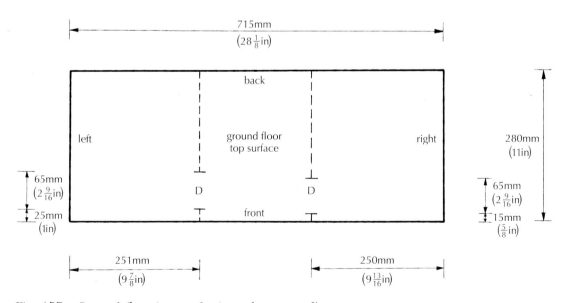

Fig. 157   Ground floor (top surface), to show screw lines.

131

the edges of the floor and back panel are correctly aligned.

(5) Drill a hole where marked in the edge of the floor panel 12mm (½in) deep, then enlarge the hole in the back panel, using the 3mm (⅛in) drill bit.

(6) Screw the back panel to the ground floor, then mark positions for the other screw destination holes.

(7) Dismantle the structure, and repeat steps 4 and 5 for the other holes.

(8) Re-screw the back to the ground floor panel.

(9) Repeat steps 3–7 for the first floor and the top floor.

Fig. 158   Sides fixed to back and floor assembly.

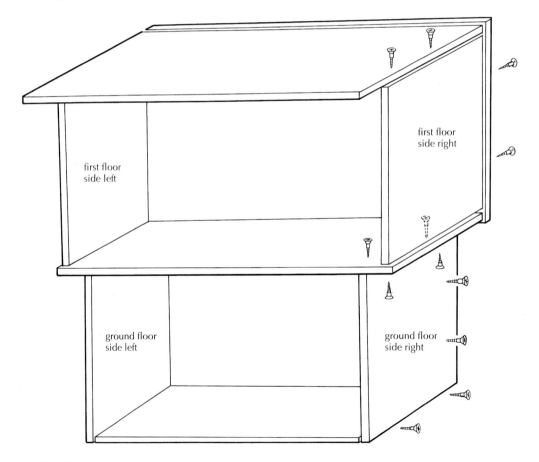

Fig. 159   Fitting house sides to back and floor assembly.

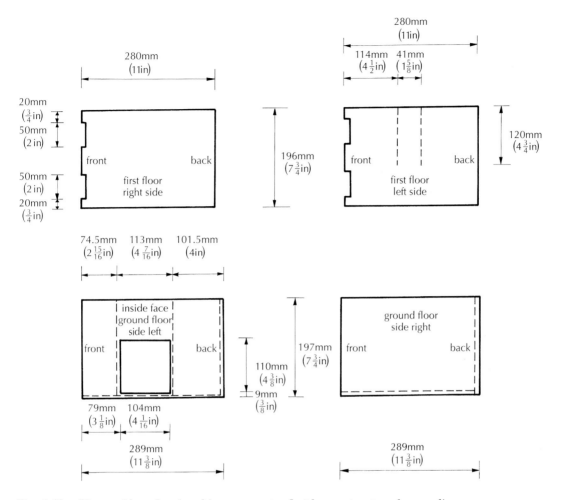

Fig. 160   House sides, showing hinge cut-outs, fireplace cut-out and screw lines.

Warning – Do not press down on the newly assembled unsupported floors at this stage, as this would tear the screws from the wood.

FIXING SIDES TO BACK AND FLOOR ASSEMBLY

Using: upper side right, upper side left, lower side right, lower side left.

Method

(1) Cut the slots for hinge fillets from the upper sides right and left.

(2) Cut and fit pieces of 12×12mm ($\frac{1}{2} \times \frac{1}{2}$in) hardwood batten into the slots, using epoxy resin adhesive. Make sure the fillets are a tight fit, and, prior to assembly, put adhesive on all bonding faces. It is particularly important that the long edge meets the edge of the cut-out slot with no dips and hollows. The hardwood fillet should be oversized and should overlap on all three sides. When the adhesive has fully cured, plane away the excess material so that the

133

hardwood fillets are flush with the panels on all sides.

(3) Trim out the fireplace hole in the left side lower panel, then mark and drill the screw lines on this and the right side lower panel (holes at 75mm/3in centres).

(4) Place the lower right side panel against the assembly in its correct position, and mark through one of the screw holes with a bradawl as before. Repeat the procedure as for fixing floors, by drilling out the screw holes, screwing the panel into place, marking other screw holes, drilling them and then finally assembling. NB Only two screws are used to fix the first floor to the top of the side panel. This is because neatly concealing screw-heads in a floor to be carved to represent floor-boards can be difficult, and since two screws will suffice, no more are used.

(5) Repeat for lower left side panel.

(6) Insert upper side right between the top floor and the first floor, mark one of the screw holes and continue in the usual way. Repeat the procedure for the upper side left panel.

CHIMNEY AND STACK

Using: front house stack, back house stack, two sloping infill strips, stack sides, front and back and filler piece, plus chimney main stack panel.

Method

(1) Trim front and back house stack pieces. They should fit against the side of the house, underneath the projecting upper jetty. Drill screw holes in the stack side pieces along one edge, as in Fig. 164.

(2) Mark and screw stack pieces to the lower side panel in the usual way, using the pre-drilled screw-line holes.

(3) Mark and screw the stack sides to the upper side panel, leaving 360mm (14¼in) projecting above the top floor.

(4) Trim the sloping infill pieces so that they fit against the surface of the main stack sides, and meet the edge of the house stack sides at an angle. Mark the outer edge of these sloping pieces on the upper panel side, remove them, drill suitable holes in the side panel, then mark, pilot-hole and screw them into position.

Fig. 161   Main side panel fixed to chimney.

Fig. 162   Sides of stack and chimney fixed to house.

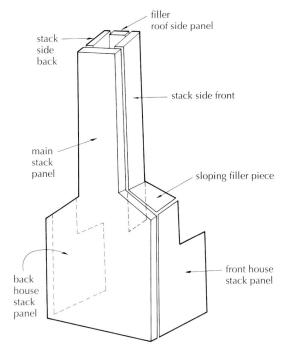

Fig. 163   Construction of chimney and stack.

(5) Place the stack infill strip between the stack sides, then mark, drill and screw it into place.

(6) Position the main side panel against the open side of the assembly, making sure that all edges overlap. Draw the outline of the assembly's outer edge on to the inside face of this panel.

(7) Trim away the overlap along this line.

(8) Use the marking gauge to measure and mark lines 4.5mm (³⁄₁₆in) inside these lines – these are screw lines, which should be drilled as such.

(9) Screw the main side panel into position as usual.

(10) Plane off or chisel away any residual overlap.

If you are making a spiral chimney top, follow the method outlined in Chapter 10, and mark a line around the stack, 755mm (29³⁄₄in) from the base. Cut away this excess material, ideally using a precision mitre saw, to produce a true edge on all four sides. Otherwise use a tenon or cross-cut

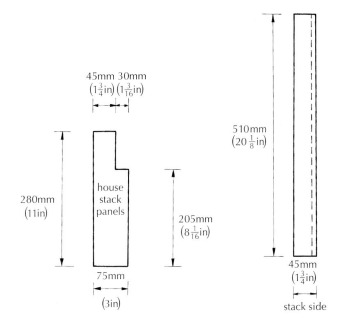

Fig. 164   Dimensions to which house stack panels should be cut, and screw lines for stack sides.

Fig. 165   Carcase with ground- and first-floor walls fitted.

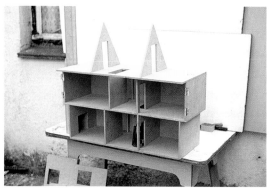

Fig. 166   House with all internal walls fitted.

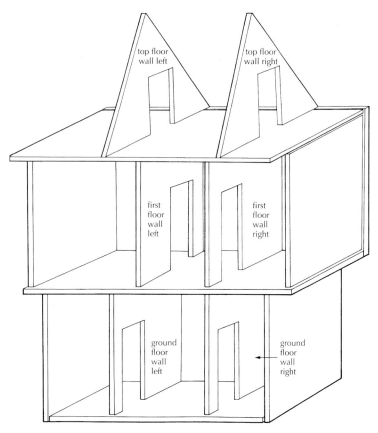

Fig. 167   Positioning of internal walls.

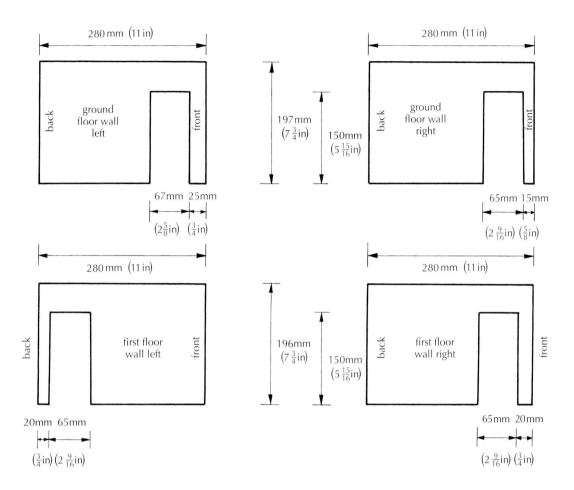

Fig. 168   Internal walls, showing door cut-outs.

saw. If you are making a shorter chimney top, cut the stack longer to compensate for this.

FITTING DIVIDING WALLS – FIRST FIX ONLY

Using: upper-floor walls left and right, middle-floor walls left and right, ground-floor walls left and right.

NB The walls are placed in position so that the screw hole lines are approximately centralised in the wall panel's thickness, then the holes are marked. Since the pilot holes are always drilled in the dead centre of the panel's edge, the screw line will be in the centre of the panel, therefore locating the wall in the right place automatically.

Method
(1) Cut upper-floor walls left and right to a triangular shape as in Fig. 169. Cut out the door apertures.

137

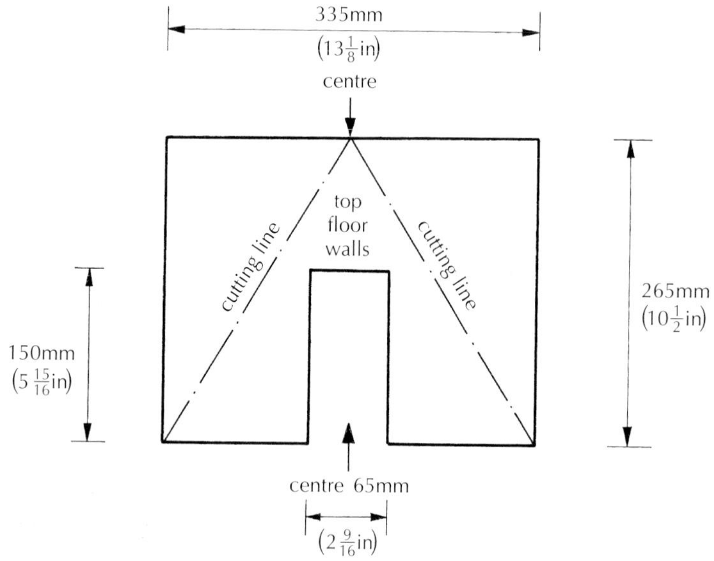
335mm
(13⅛in)
centre
top
floor
walls
cutting line
cutting line
265mm
(10½in)
150mm
(5 15/16in)
centre 65mm
(2 9/16in)

Fig. 169 Top floor walls, showing door cut-outs and final shape.

(2) Cut out the door apertures for the remaining four walls.
(3) Fit the right first floor wall, screwing it into place.
(4) Fit the right lower wall beneath it. It is impossible to screw its top to the underside of the first floor, but when finally assembled, gluing alone will hold it in place.
(5) Fit the left lower wall, using only two screws, front and back, so as not to disfigure the plywood surface unnecessarily.
(6) Fit the remaining walls.

OPENING FRONT SECTIONS

These are made to overlap by chamfering the mating edges, as explained in Chapter 6. The main Front Section Left (FSL) closes beneath the smaller Front Section Right (FSR), which overlaps it.

Using: FSR panel, FSL panel, four strips (width 34mm/1⅜in) for FSR, and four strips (width 34mm/1⅜in) and one strip (width 40mm/1⅝in) for FSL, FSR frontplate (6mm/¼in MDF) and FSL front plate (also 6mm/¼in MDF), window rebate infill pieces for both sections (eight in total).

Method

(1) Establish the front break line (FBL) at the front of the house structure, by measuring 263mm (10 5/16in) from the right-hand side at the top, and marking this distance underneath the overlap on the top floor. Then measure 233mm (9 3/16in) from the right-hand side at the bottom, and mark this point on the front of the edge of the ground floor. Once these points are marked, check with a try square that the line joining these two points is at right angles to the floors. If there is a minor discrepancy, alter one of the marks so that the line is exactly at right angles to the floors – this is more important than precise measurments.
(2) Refer to the method in Chapter 6, but do not hang the doors before chamfering the edges, since the jetty over-

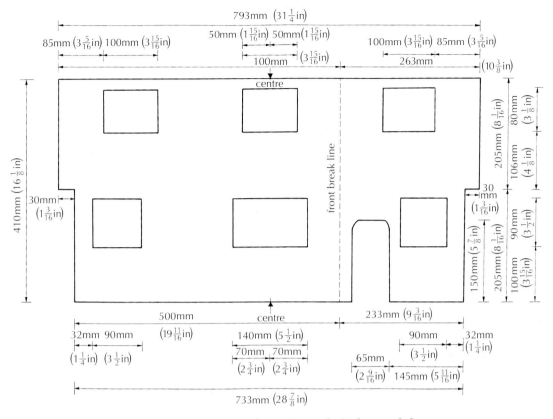

Fig. 170   Opening front sections, showing dimensions of window and door cut-outs.

hang makes this tricky. Instead, chamfer the doors first, and plane away material until the doors meet neatly on the FBL. Chamfer material from the *front* of FSL, and from the *back* of FSR.

(3) With both panels held against the front of the house, their meeting edges overlapping at the FBL as they should, draw lines to mark the panels' overlap to the right and left of the house front, on the backs of the panels, then trim away the waste.

(4) Rebate the hinges into the hardwood fillets in the upper side panels, 25mm (1in) from top and bottom, then hang the FSR and FSL so that

the panels close together as they should.

(5) Cut out the window and door holes.

(6) Remove FSR and FSL from the house.

(7) Mark and drill the screw lines in the usual way.

(8) For FSL, trim away the section of the long top strip, then screw it along the top of the panel, with the cut-out section at the front and to the left – this will accommodate the 6mm (¼in) thick front plate.

(9) Screw the side strips and bottom strip into position, then do the same with the strip at the right-hand side, fixing this beside the curve, 9mm (⅜in) away from the right-hand edge.

139

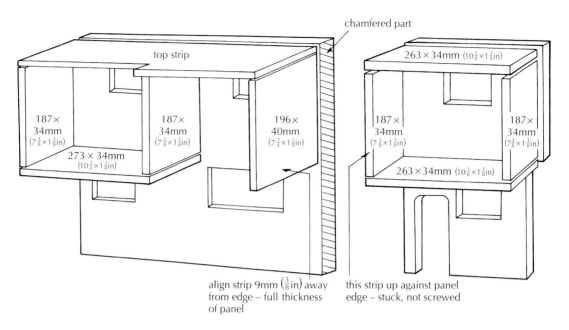

Fig. 171 Arrangement of strips on FSL and FSR.

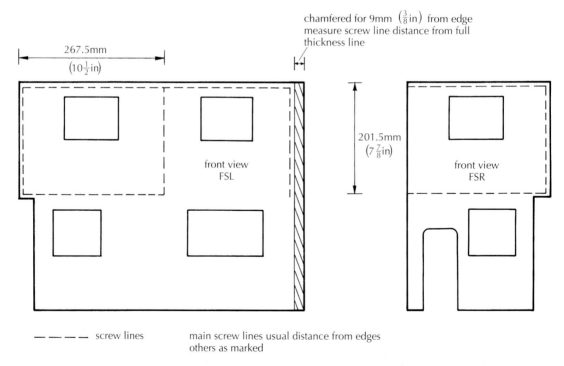

Fig. 172 Screw lines for FSL and FSR to facilitate fitting of strips.

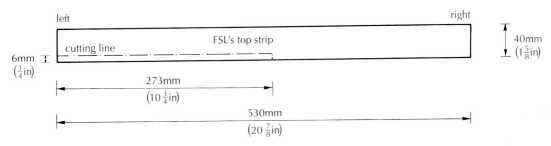

Fig. 173   Trimming of FSL's top strip to allow for affixing of front plate.

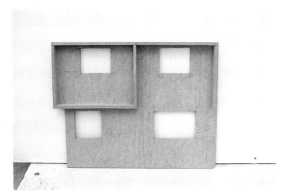

Fig. 174   FSL with strips added.

Fig. 175   Clamping and gluing left-hand strip to front of FSR.

Fig. 176   FSR with top and side strips fitted.

(10) For FSR, screw the top, bottom and right side strips on to the panel as for the FSL, then clamp and glue the left-hand strip in place, using no screws (these would not hold in the sloping panel).

(11) Fit and screw the front plates on to the strips.

(12) Dismantle the structure (excluding FSR right-hand strip), marking the

141

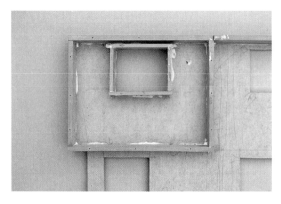

Fig. 177   Gluing window cavity infill strip on to FSL.

pieces for reassembly. Countersink all the host screw holes, then glue and reassemble the panels and strips, without adding the front plates.

(13) Glue the cavity strip infill pieces (6mm/¼in thickness) around the edges of the window apertures on FSR and FSL, then screw and glue the front plates into position, first applying glue to the other edges of the infill pieces.

(14) Re-hang the opening front sections and check that they close properly. Plane away any obtruding pieces of timber.

MAKING THE ROOF – MAIN STRUCTURE

Using: two main roof panels, base, hipped roof end panels, left and right side, closers, triangular support pieces and 9 × 9mm (⅜ × ⅜in) batten, roof base.

Method

(1) Cut the main roof panels to shape.

(2) Draw a line along the centre of the roof base lengthways, also marking it on the underside. Measure and mark lines 195mm (7¹¹⁄₁₆in) away from this line, on its top surface. Tap nails or panel pins along these lines, only enough to hold the structure, as they are for temporary support.

(3) Slightly chamfer the inner top edges of the main roof panels. Place them on the base with their top edges together and the lower edges resting against the nails or pins. Ensure that the ridge line (where they meet) is directly above the centre line marked on the base, at both ends. The distance between the centre line of the base and the top of the ridge should be approximately 260mm (10¼in). Ensure that the ruler is held at right angles to the base.

Fig. 178   FSL and FSR. Re-hung on to front of house and closed.

Fig. 179   Front sections fixed to house and open.

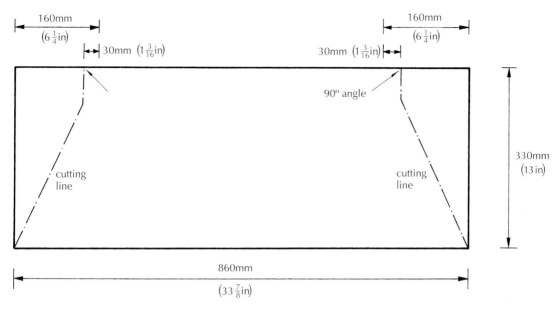

Fig. 180   Dimensions of main roof panels.

(4) With the panels balanced in this way, place the bevel gauge over the ridge and adjust it so that its angle precisely matches that of the roof.

(5) Use the bevel gauge, still set to this angle, to mark the angle of cut for the triangular support pieces (9mm/⅜in MDF). Measure down from the apex of the triangle approximately 120mm (4⅜in), and join the lines. Cut along the lines.

(6) Dismantle the roof panel assembly and mark lines inside each panel for the triangular supports, 80mm (3⅛in) from each end (*see* Chapter 7). Drill host screw holes along these lines and screw and glue the panels to the supports, firstly countersinking the host screw holes. NB Take care when countersinking 6mm (¼in) thick MDF, as it is easy to drill too deeply and tear through the thickness altogether, or leave too thin a piece to support the screw-head properly.

(7) Using screws in suitable positions, glue strips of 9 × 9mm (⅜ × ⅜in) batten along the lower edge (eaves) of both panels. Clamp the batten in place until the glue has set. If you would rather screw the batten in place, remove the screws after the glue has dried.

(8) Plane away the outside angle of the exposed batten, so that the base fits against the eaves of the panels, with only a slight gap between the eaves and the base's surface.

(9) Screw and glue the base to the battens and thus to the eaves of the panels, making sure that it is fixed centrally. The best method is to mark the centre of the base and of the roof panels widthways and line these up, at the same time lining up the base centre line with the ridge apex above.

(10) Trim the base overlaps at both ends. Cut and then plane away the overlap at the front and back (eaves),

143

finishing off by matching the angle of the base's edge with that of the slope of the roof, so that the base continues this same slope.

(11) Screw and glue 9 × 9mm (⅜ × ⅜in) battens at each end of the base. Use 19mm (¾in) length screws.

(12) Screw and glue battens inside the open ends of the roof panels, as a way of joining the hip slope panels of the roof on to it.

(13) For each end, place a hip slope panel over the open area, butting its top against the lower side of the gablet's angle (bottom side of the triangle).

(14) Draw a line around the two roof slope sides, to mark the excess material. Trim this away.

(15) Screw and glue the hip slope panels in position, then trim and plane away excess material so that the edge's angle follows that of the main roof slope.

(16) Glue and clamp battens inside the open area of the gablet (top of the roof). Then screw and glue oversized pieces of 6mm (¼in) MDF over these triangular holes and trim and plane away excess material.

(17) Screw and glue battens on to the inside of the base edges of the hip panels. When the glue is dry, remove the screws.

(18) Plane away the corner along the length of the batten material until this timber's plane is flush with the base of the main roof panels.

(19) Screw and glue the roof base on to the base of the roof assembly, screwing into the battens that were planed in step 18.

(20) Trim and plane the excess material of the base panel until its edges follow the slope of the main roof panels.

(21) Cut out the central area of the base

Fig. 181   Battens glued in place to receive hip slope panel.

Fig. 182   Drilling pilot holes for fixing oversize panel over hole.

Fig. 183   Screwing panels on to batten.

Fig. 184   Roof in place on the house.

Fig. 186   Tiling hip slope up to where angle changes.

Fig. 185   Clamping tile strips to main panel – only required if strips pull away.

Fig. 187   Showing measurement marks on roof to give even tiling.

roof panels, leaving a 70mm (2⅝in) width around the perimeter.

(22) Trim out slots to allow for the two upper-storey (triangular) room walls.

TILING THE ROOF

Follow the procedure outlined in Chapter 7 for making roof tiles using plywood. Where the hips of the roof meet at an angle, and at the ridge, use air-hardening clay rolled into cylindrical shapes and stuck

Fig. 188   Both angles of hip slope tiled.

on to the lines to create ridge and saddle-back tiles, marking the joint lines of these as necessary. Remember to first apply PVA adhesive to the wood and MDF so that the clay will stick.

FINAL FIX AND ADDING EXTERNAL FEATURES

INTERNAL DECORATIONS

(1) Make all interior doors of the correct size and according to your chosen style, and decorate them.

(2) Remove all interior walls from the structure, then hang all interior doors, so that they open in a convenient way – as far as possible avoiding causing obstructions in narrow areas.

(3) Dismantle the remainder of the structure, marking all the pieces (including interior walls) for reassembly. Remember that walls, floors and ceilings will be decorated before reassembly, so mark panels on edges that are not going to be painted; that is those that will be bonded to other panels. Mark in more than one place in case one marking is inadvertently obliterated. Remove interior doors from walls, and mark them underneath for refitting.

(4) Decorate, according to taste, *both sides* of the interior walls (prototype – white emulsion), the *inside* faces of the external wall panels (prototype as interior walls). The ceiling of the first floor and the floor of the top floor are the underside and top side respectively of the same panel, and for the prototype the top side was left plain (for later addition of floorboards) and the underside was emulsioned

Fig. 189   *Scraping off paint to facilitate gluing.*

white. In the same way, the first floor and the ground-floor ceiling are both sides of the same panel, and for the prototype the top surface was carved to represent floorboards (*see* Chapter 12) and its underside (ground-floor ceiling) emulsioned white.

(5) Use a small chisel to scrape away dried paint (or varnish for carved and varnished floorboards) from any areas where edges of boards are to be bonded. Also sand away paint or varnish from the edges which are to be bonded. PVA glue will only successfully stick bare timber or MDF.

(6) Countersink all the host screw holes on their outside (screw's entry) side.

(7) Re-hang doors to the internal walls.

(8) Screw and glue the complete house structure together. You may find that when the main structure is firmly screwed and glued together, the interior walls are impossible to fit, because the structure has altered slightly. In this event, plane away any excess material until the walls fit correctly. Also, the right-hand ground-floor wall cannot be screwed from

above, as the right first-floor wall is on top of the screw line. Gluing is perfectly adequate for fixing this in place.

(9) Screw and glue the chimney assembly on to the left-hand wall.

(10) Plane and/or chisel away material from the front edges of the walls until the house front presents a smooth level plane, against which the front sections can fit.

ADDING BEAMS AND WINDOW DETAILS

Refer to Chapter 9 for the method of fixing beams.

Using: FSR and FSL, 6mm (¼in) cell-size metal mesh, 12 × 6mm (½ × ¼in), 12 × 12mm (½ × ½in), and 6 × 6mm (¼ × ¼in) batten, offcuts of 9mm (⅜in) MDF for jetty struts under the jetty and curving beams.

Windows

(1) Following the instructions in Chapter 8, rebate shallow grooves around the window apertures for the window mesh. (The prototype was diamond-shaped – you may prefer a square shape or another type of window bar altogether.)

(2) Cut suitable sizes of metal mesh to fit the enlarged window apertures, or alternatively make up metal window lattices of appropriate sizes. Use contact adhesive to glue them in place.

(3) Screw FSR and FSL into place on the house front, making sure that they close correctly. Trim away any tight-fitting areas.

(4) Fit a screw hook and eye, or magnetic catch fastening, as a way of fastening the FSR to the underside of the first floor.

Fig. 190   Cutting a groove for windows.

Fig. 191   Beaming for FSL partially complete.

Beaming for FSL – Top Left (Upper Jetty) Section

Place the house flat on a bench or table, so that the front is uppermost. Where no size is given, the beam batten size is 12 × 6mm (½ × ¼in). All other beam sizes are stipulated.

Vertical = v
Horizontal = h
Slanted = s

The order of gluing on the beams is as follows:

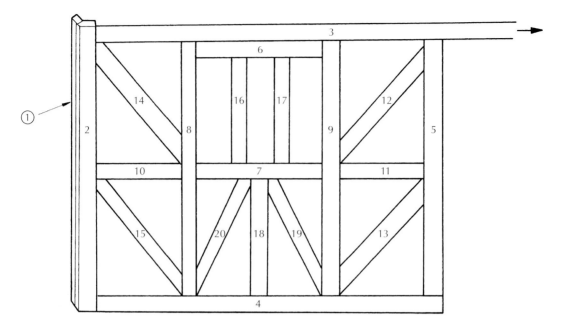

Fig. 192   FSL top section – beam arrangement.

1 (v) (6 × 6mm/¼ × ¼in) along the left-hand side edge of the panel, its front flush with FSL front.
2 (v) on the front left-hand edge of the panel, glued partly to the front of 1, and partly to the panel's surface.
3 (h) right along the top edge of entire FSL, half of it bonded to the 9mm (⅜in) edge of the MDF top strip and extending to the end of this, and
4 (h) along the bottom edge of only top left section.
5 (v) between 3 and 4.
6 (h) (6 × 6mm/¼ × ¼in) top of window, the exact width of the window opening (100mm/4in), bonded to the underside of 3.
7 (h) (12 × 12mm/½ × ½in) window sill, also 100mm (4in).
8 (v) between 3 and 4, upper section acting as left side of window frame.
9 (v) between 3 and 4, upper section acting as right side of window frame.

10 (h) between 2 and 8, running parallel with 7, and
11 (h) between 9 and 5, also parallel with 7.
12 (s) cut to correct angle at both ends, top end against 5, bottom end against 9.
13 (s) as 12.
14 and 15 (both s) positioned between 2 and 8 in the same way as 12 and 13 are between 5 and 9.
16 and
17 (both v) window bars, to divide the window equally into 3. Stuck at the ends to 6 and 7 (accurate cutting required).
18, 19 and 20 between 8 and 9.

Beaming for FSL – Right Top Section
The order of gluing on the beams is as follows:

1 (h) parallel with 4 from top left section, spanning the distance between

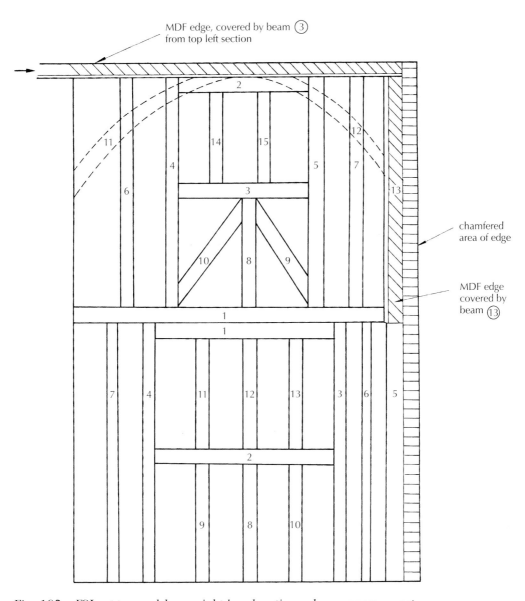

Fig. 193   FSL upper and lower right-hand section – beam arrangement.

right side of jetty outcrop wall and left of right side strip.

2 (h) top side of window, and

3 (h) $(12 \times 12\text{mm}/\frac{1}{2} \times \frac{1}{2}\text{in})$ as window sill. Both should be the exact size of window width (100mm/4in).

4 and

5 (both v) positioned either side of the window.

6 and 7 (both v) fixed mid-way between the spaces on the wall either side of the window frame.

8 (v) underneath the window sill, dividing the panel area in two.

149

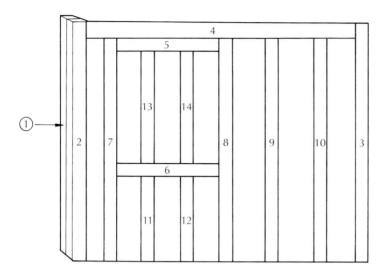

Fig. 194   FSL left-hand lower section.

9 and 10 (both s) dividing the rectangular areas bounded by 8, 3, 5 and 1, and 4, 3, 8 and 1 respectively.

11 and 12 are curved strut pieces cut from 9mm (⅜in) MDF. To make these, cut a rectangle 100 × 95mm (4 × 3¾in). With the 95mm (3¾in) side uppermost, draw a gentle curve to join the bottom left and top right corner. Cut this curve, then sand away any harsh angles. Use dividers to measure and mark a distance of 17mm (⅝in) above this line, then cut along it. Use this strut as a tem-

Fig. 195   FSL lower section beaming.

plate to mark the other. Stick the struts in place, their front faces aligning with the front edges of the MDF strips.

13 (v) down front of right-hand MDF strip.

14 and 15 (both v) window bars.

Beaming for Left-Hand Lower Section of FSL

The order of gluing on the beams is as follows:

1 (v) (6 × 6mm/¼ × ¼in) on the left-hand side edge, butting up to the underside of the jetty projection and continuing to the ground.

2 (v) on the front side left-hand edge, partly against 1 and partly against the front panel; length should be the same as 1.

3 (v) in line with right-hand side of edge of top section, parallel with the vertical timber above it.

4 (h) spanning the distance between 3 and 2, underneath the jetty overhang, stuck against the panel.

5 (h) (6 × 6mm/¼ × ¼in) upper window frame, 90mm (3½in) long, and

150

6 (h) $(12 \times 12\text{mm}/\frac{1}{2} \times \frac{1}{2}\text{in})$ lower window sill, of the same length.

7 (v) butting against 4 at the top and going to the ground, forming left-hand side of window frame.

8 (v), as 7, but on the right-hand side of window.

9 and 10 (both v) divide the distance between 3 and 8 equally into 3 areas.

11 and 12 (both v) divide the area between 7 and 8 (below the window) equally into 3 areas.

13 and 14 (both v) divide the window vertically, and are in line with 11 and 12.

Fig. 196   Close-up of struts under joist end pieces.

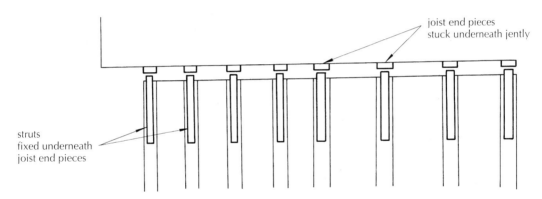

Fig. 197   Arrangement of jetty struts and joist end pieces for FSL, FSR and house sides.

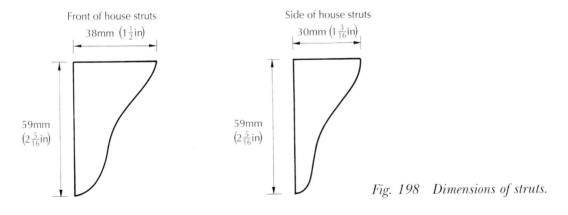

Fig. 198   Dimensions of struts.

151

Stick them at the ends against the top of the window and its sill (accurate cutting is required).

Jetty Struts and Joist End Pieces

Stick joist end pieces underneath the jetty outcrop. Place them in line and at right angles to the vertical posts below. Cut the eight front panel struts from 9mm (⅜in) MDF and stick these underneath the pieces and against the joists below.

Completing a Dragon Post by Joining Adjacent Jetty Struts at Corners

Where the corner jetty struts on FSL and FSR meet, a dragon post can be formed by filling the void between them with air-hardening clay and shaping this into a curve.

(1) Make a clay 'comb' by marking the widest distance between the two struts on to a piece of thin plywood or MDF and cutting a gentle curve between these lines. This can be used to smooth the clay to a rounded shape.

(2) Apply PVA adhesive to the MDF surfaces.

(3) Apply clay, small pieces at a time, pushing it hard into the corner until it is slightly proud of the outer edges of the jetty strips either side.

(4) Comb the clay with the tool made in step 1, to remove surplus material.

(5) Mark with a nail or modelling tool as required.

Right-Hand Lower Section of FSL

The order of gluing on the beams is as follows:

1 (h) underneath the beam above and to act as upper window frame, the exact width of the window – 140mm (5⅜in).

Fig. 199   Comb held to show curve.

Fig. 200   Clay applied proud of surface.

Fig. 201   Comb smoothing off excess clay.

Fig. 202   Smooth dragon post formed.

Fig. 203 Dragon post marked with grooves.

Fig. 204   Beaming complete on FSR.

2 (h) (12 × 12mm/½ × ½in) window sill –
140mm (5½in).

3 (v) from underneath above beam to
the ground, acting as right-hand
window frame.

4 (v) as above, acting as left-hand window
frame.

5 (v) parallel with 3 and 4, at right-hand
edge, in line with the strip above. NB
Ensure that the positioning of this
beam does not interfere with the
opening and closing of FSL.

6 (v) parallel with the others, placed
mid-way along the panel area.

7 (v) as above, also dividing the panel
area in half.

8 (v) below the window sill, dividing the
area equally in two.

9 (v) as above, mid-way between 8 and
4.

10 (v) as above, mid-way between 8 and
3.

11, 12 and 13 are window bars, bonded
above at their ends to 1 and 2, dividing the window areas equally, and in
line with 9, 8 and 10 respectively.

FSR – Top Section
As top section for FSL.

FSR – Lower Section
The order of gluing on the beams is as
follows:

153

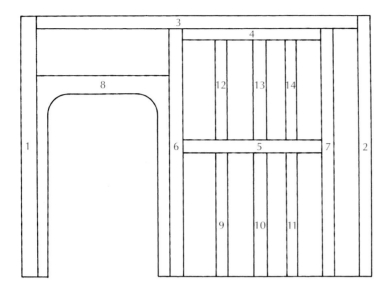

Fig. 205   FSR lower section – beam arrangement.

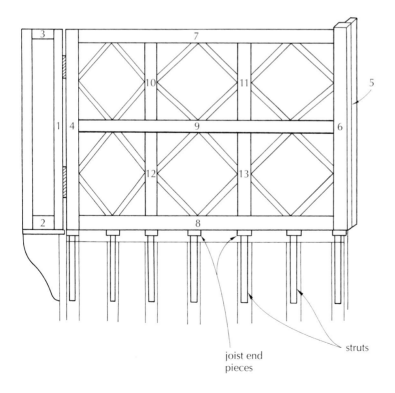

joist end
pieces

struts

Fig. 206   Right side of house – beam arrangement.

1 (v) from underneath jetty to ground.
2 (v) as above, right-hand side.
3 (h) underneath jetty between 1 and 2.
4 (h) (6 × 6mm/¼ × ¼in) top of window, fixed against and underneath 3, the exact width of the window – 90mm (3½in).
5 (h) window sill, width as above.
6 and 7 (both v) either side of window.
8 (panel) 6mm (¼in) MDF panel cut out to surround the door frame and fill the gap between the frame and the vertical timbers.

9, 10 and 11 (all v) equidistantly placed along panel.
12, 13 and
14 (all v) dividing the window.

Right Side of House – Upper Part
The order of gluing on the beams is as follows:
1 (v) (6 × 6mm/¼ × ¼in) stuck on to edge of FSR, in line with corresponding corner beam below.
2 (h) between 1 and beam at front of FSR at base, and

Fig. 207   Marking beams for cutting.

Fig. 209   Beaming right side upper section.

Fig. 208   Sticking diagonal beams within square areas on right side of the house.

Fig. 210   Close-up of beaming right side upper section.

Fig. 211   Front of house without roof – beaming completed.

3 (h) between these same beams at the top.

4 (v) top to bottom left-hand side, front edge flush with wall of house. Cut out rebates for the hinges.

5 (v) (6 × 6mm/¼ × ¼in) stuck on to back of the house in the usual way, one edge flush with the side edge, so that

6 (v) can be stuck on to side of the house, half fixed to panel and half fixed to 5.

7 (h) across the top, between 4 and 6.

8 (h) across the bottom between 4 and 6.

Fig. 212   Front view of house with roof beaming and ridge tiles completed.

Fig. 213   Corner view of house with roof beaming and tiling completed.

9 (h) between 4 and 6, mid-way between the two.

10 and 11 (both v) between 7 and 9, dividing the area into three.

12 and

13 (both v) in line with 10 and 11, between 9 and 8.

6 × 6mm (¼ × ¼in) pieces (s) positioned within the square panels so formed, to form diamond shapes.

Right Side of House – Lower Panel

Stick vertical beams in place, as detailed for FSL and FSR lower sections.

Stick joist end short pieces and struts against the vertical beams in the usual way.

Chimney Side of House

The order of gluing on the beams is as follows:

1 (v)   (6 × 6mm/¼ × ¼in)   along   top section of FSL alongside hinges.

2 and

3 (h) between 1 and front beam.

4 (v) (6 × 6mm/¼ × ¼in) along back of the house but flush with the side, and

5 (v) stuck on to the side at the left, partly on panel, partly on 4.

6 (v) at the front, flush with front of the house, with areas for hinges rebated out.

7 and 8 (both h) running along the top edge, between 5 and chimney stack and chimney stack and 6, respectively.

9 and 10 (both h) along bottom edge of jetty overhang, and, as with 7 and 8, between the chimney stack and edge beams.

11 and 12(both h) running parallel with previous four beams, dividing the area equally in two.

157

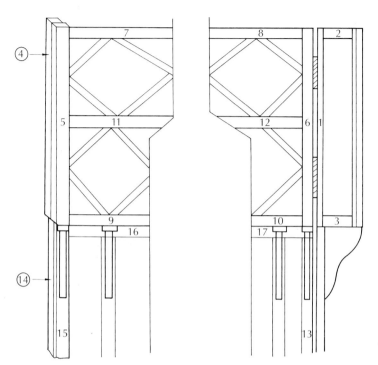

Fig. 214   Chimney side of house – beam arrangement.

13 (v) at the front edge of lower section, tight underneath jetty overhang at the top and going to the base.

14 (v) (6 × 6mm/¼ × ¼in) stuck on to the back side, front edge flush with the side, so that

15 (v) can bond to it and the panel at its left-hand edge.

16 and 17 (both h) tucking underneath jetty overhang, joining chimney stack to beams 15 and 13.

Vertical beams, joist ends and struts fitted as for right-hand side.

6 × 6mm (¼in × ¼in) (s) diagonally-laid pieces, fixed as shown in the diagram. Four laid within each of the three squares formed by:

11, 5, 7 and stack
12, stack, 8 and 6
11, stack, 9 and 5

And two laid between the square formed by:

12, 6, 10 and stack

Back

Divide the back horizontally with a large timber, with ordinary horizontal timbers at top and bottom, then add vertical timbers so as to divide the areas equally.

Finally, chisel the timbers as described in Chapter 9, then paint the exterior according to taste.

INDEX